classics

ROCKPORT

First published in the United States of America by
Rockport Publishers, Inc.
33 Commercial Street
Gloucester, Massachusetts 01930-5089
Telephone: (978) 282-9590
Facsimile: (978) 283-2742
www.rockpub.com

ISBN 1-56496-829-4

10 9 8 7 6 5 4 3 2 1

Design: Stoltze Design
Cover Images: The Futon Shop, (top); Museum of Modern Art, (second row, left; sixth row);
Tekno, (second row, right; seventh row); Retromodern.com, (third row); Paul Warchol, (fifth row).
Photo Research: Wendy Missan

Contributing Writers:
Classic Chairs: Julia Lewis
Classic Lounging: David Carlson
Classic Tables: Julia Lewis
Classic Beds: Diana Friedman
Classic Lighting: Kira L. Gould
Classic Storage and Accessories: Bonnie Schwartz
Additional Text: Ann Kirby Payne

Printed in China.

# Introduction

Just as fashion has the little black dress, pearls, and the Kelly bag, interior design has its own classics. These simple elements are what professional designers count on to pull a room together. From the four-poster bed to the Eames lounge chair, each creates a design statement that is straightforward and stylish. Once the province of interior designers, the classics are now readily available—through magazines, Web sites, and catalogues. Authentic classics, and even some good looking knock-offs have migrated from the to-the-trade-only showrooms to retail shops. As mainstream America becomes more educated and design savvy, readers want design advice that is sensible, easy to use, and tasteful. Each chapter in this book includes a look at design classics in the areas of furniture, lighting, seating, sofas, beds, and accessories. The décor elements and featured advice are both time-honored and design-tried-and-true. And, here, time-honored doesn't mean time-worn: the book is fresh, innovative, and knows how to use great pieces to wake up a room.

Classic elements shown through close-ups, details, and images of complete room designs and sidebars will help you choose and use the pieces that are right for you. In addition, boxed text offers practical, concrete interior design information about adopting design classics to create a particular look or atmosphere. In the pages you will find simple, affordable design (classics with staying power) and interior design advice and inspiration, all in an easy-to-use format (element by element) that looks and feels fresh and up-to-date.

# classic chairs

Emeco 1006 Chair

Bertoia Chair

Saarinen's Womb Chair

Thonet Bentwood Chair

Barcelona Chair

Oval X-Back Chair

Cesca Chair

Club Chair

Windsor Chair

Eames DCM

∧ FLEXIBLE STYLE

The magic of the Emeco chair: It looks as equally at home with contemporary furnishings as it does with simple, flea-market finds. Here, pulled up to 1950s retro table draped with a color-saturated tablecloth and decorated with a bouquet of exotic flowers, the chairs transform a plain kitchen table into a more elegant dining surface.

< CONTRAST

Update a country look by pairing Emeco chairs with a pine farm table; the contrast of the sleek, aluminum finish with soft pine tempers the saccharine side of country style.

# Decorating with the Ideal Chair

Built of a durable but extremely lightweight aluminum alloy, the Emeco chair is made to last the millennia.

DIMENSIONS: H 34 IN. (86 CM) x D 19.5 IN. (50 CM) x W 16.5 IN. (42 CM)

## WHAT MAKES IT CLASSIC

- *PERFECT DINING CHAIR:* The Emeco chair is the perfect dining chair for a family with children, looking for indestructible furniture; it is durable enough to support more than three times the weight of a comparable steel chair.

- *DESIGNERS' FAVORITE:* Design pros such as Frank Gehry, Philippe Starck, and Ettore Sottsass admired this sturdy and unadorned chair so much that it found its way into their work, and then eventually into interiors around the world.

- *ORIGINS:* Originally called the "Navy Chair" or "Prison Chair," the Emeco 1006 was developed to meet the specifications of the United States Navy for use on ships, and later became standard issue in state hospitals and federal penitentiaries.

Squared, curved, and contoured, the Emeco 1006 represents the essence of what it is to be a chair. With its four squared-off legs, contoured seat, and curved back reinforced by three vertical stretchers, it seems conjured by someone asked to imagine the ideal image of a chair. Though it looks sleek and somewhat modest, it is made to last the millennia with a durable but extremely lightweight aluminum alloy, which is non-flammable, non-magnetic, and non-corrosive. Formed, welded, ground, annealed, heat-treated, and finished, the one-piece construction can support more than three times the weight of a comparable steel chair and withstand the most punishing use.

### A HARD-WORKING CHAIR

Heavy duty, but lightweight, the style of Emeco may be all things to all people: It works with everything from an antique pine farm table to a modern glass-top dining table. It can also stand up well against many backdrops—you'll find the Emeco looking handsome in restaurants and right at home in residential interiors for families with children.

The Emeco chair doesn't fight with the décor or table it's paired with—its quiet, clean lines mix easily with other styles. To heat up a contemporary dining room, couple these chairs with a smooth, wood-top table in light tones, such as maple or birch—the bright warmth of the wood tones contrast beautifully with the cool, brushed aluminum finish.

While the original model was produced as a dining-height side chair with an indestructible natural anodized aluminum finish, today Emeco also manufactures armed, upholstered, and counter-height versions. In recent years, Emeco introduced a spectrum of playful, colored finishes that soften the more sober, industrial look of aluminum.

The Bertoia side chair's delicate wire mesh frame gives back space to a small home or apartment.

DIMENSIONS: H 30 IN. (76 CM) x D 19.75 IN. (50 CM) x W 21.75 IN. (55 CM)

### WHAT MAKES IT CLASSIC

- *SPACE-SAVING SEATING: Look to the Bertoia Wire Side Chair as space-saving seating for furnishing a small apartment or house: It easily slides under a dining table for a compact profile; and its thin metal legs and wire mesh seat are almost transparent, reducing its presence to give back inches to a cramped space.*

- *ORIGINS: Harry Bertoia worked closely with Charles and Ray Eames on their groundbreaking experiments with molded plywood furniture in California, but broke away in the late 1940s to concentrate on his interest in the properties of metal and the development of chair forms that respond to the requirements of the human body—efforts that led to the wire mesh and organic form of the Bertoia Wire Side chair.*

> ADDED SPACE
> The wire mesh back of the Bertoia Wire Side chair allows it to practically disappear, visually adding space to a small kitchen or dining room. Red seat pads add a splash of color to a monochromatic, modern table setting.

# Wired for Elegance

The Bertoia chair is a perennial favorite, with its lithe, sculptural form. Its distinct silhouette provides a light, elegant alternative to bulky, upholstered furniture. In addition, its see-through frame filters light and casts lively shadows on surrounding surfaces. Choose from an array of solid color seat pads to coordinate with your home décor and palette.

### THE CHAIR YOU CAN SEE THROUGH

Praised by design press and professionals alike, Bertoia's simple side chair is characterized by a contoured, open grid of welded steel rods with chrome or nylon-dipped finishes. The Bertoia chair with a seat pad is ideal for furnishing an open-plan living room or dining room, where bulkier, upholstered furniture obstructs sight lines from one space to another. For small homes with compartmentalized rooms, its sleighlike thin metal legs enhance long views from living room to dining room to kitchen. Decorate with this chair to maximize natural light in your home.

Pair Bertoia chairs with a glass-, marble-, or laminate-topped dining room table for a clean, modern style. In small spaces, such as a small kitchen or dining room, group them around a simple, round, pedestal dining table. If you prefer to personalize your dining room with a more eclectic look, pull them up to a wooden country table—the light, sculptural shape of the chrome chair frames provide a striking contrast to the substantial bulk of a wood table. Keep in mind that the chair's sleigh base works best with table bases of a similar shape.

### PATIO PERFECT

One of the most popular and ubiquitous of Bertoia's furniture designs, the side chair can be used as a dining chair inside the house or on the patio. Animated by its gridded, sculptural form, with removable upholstered cushions, rust-resistant finish, and latticed form that allows drainage, the chair was intended for all-weather outdoor, as well as indoor use. Indeed, the Bertoia chair appears in New York's Museum of Modern Art Sculpture Garden and nearby Paley Park.

∧ RELAXED STYLE
Play up the relaxed style of a Womb chair by covering it in a textured, neutral fabric that will work in any comfortable, California-style interior. Wood coffee table base, stool, and Chinese chair provide a patina of age that adds warmth and history to the room. Add touches of brighter color through flowers, pillows, and accessories.

< THE PERFECT COMPLEMENT
The Womb chair is the perfect complement to the standard upholstered sofa and arm chair in this small and eclectic modern living room. Upholstered in a playful, patterned design whose red keys into the storage wall behind, it doesn't have the bulky shape of an uphol-stered arm chair. Instead, its delicate metal legs and curved shape visually open up a living room corner.

A trim yet comfortable alternative to the traditional arm chair.

DIMENSIONS: H 35.5 IN. (90 CM) x D 34 IN. (86 CM) x W 40 IN. (102 CM)

## WHAT MAKES IT CLASSIC

- *RELAXED AND BEAUTIFUL STYLE: With its enveloping contours and a big, cup-like shell where you can curl up and read, sip coffee, or just relax, the Womb chair offers emotional comfort as well as physical retreat. Place it in a quiet corner of a bedroom or study to take full advantage of its relaxed, comfortable style.*

- *ORIGINS: Architect Eero Saarinen, another colleague of Charles and Ray Eames in their efforts at molding plywood, embraced the possibilities of mass production with molded fiberglass during the 1940s—the wide flared upholstered piece that is known as the Womb chair was Saarinen's breakthrough design.*

# The Armchair Reborn

The Womb chair is the modern, comfortable answer to the traditional, overstuffed, high-back chair. Made of a thin, molded-fiberglass shell padded with foam and supported by delicate tubular metal legs, the chair expresses a relaxed and casual lifestyle that we associate with contemporary living.

This graceful, commodious chair is a flattering backdrop for the sitter; it is also a beautiful object by itself, so make sure you position the chair with enough visual space to emphasize its sculptural qualities. Its cup-shape design also allows this piece to fit harmoniously into the corner of a living room, study, or even a bedroom, providing an ideal place for lounging or reading.

With the help of upholstery, you can tailor this typically modern, organic-shaped chair to coordinate with your style of home décor: Cover it in a bright solid red or blue fabric, or in lively, patterned upholstery to coordinate with a color-rich, contemporary decorative scheme. Don't be afraid to mix the smooth shell shape of the Womb chair with the irregular lines of your favorite antiques, such as an old farm table cut down as a coffee table, folk stools, or carved side tables—the contrasting textures and forms create a pleasing counterpoint.

These willowy chairs exceed expectations as the strong, graphic curves lend the century-old designs an unexpectedly modern feel.

DIMENSIONS: H 32 IN. (81.3 CM) X D 20 IN. (51 CM) X W 18 IN. (45.7 CM)

### WHAT MAKES IT CLASSIC

- *STRENGTH IN STYLE: Graceful and timeless, bentwood chairs are for the ages. Their lyrical silhouettes work remarkably well with modern interiors, yet their historic form makes them a natural for more traditional rooms. A choice of caned or upholstered seats, ranging from natural to dark and exotic, make it possible to find a bentwood chair to suit any space.*

- *STRENGTH IN SUBSTANCE: Lightweight yet surprisingly strong, bentwood chairs can withstand heavy use, making them ideal for dining rooms and kitchens.*

- *ORIGINS: During the mid-nineteenth century, patriarch Michael Thonet refined wood-bending techniques for the mass production of high-quality, inexpensive, modern furniture. Many of today's most popular bentwood chair designs date back to the late-nineteenth and early-twentieth centuries.*

# Classic Curves

With their flowing curves and delicate lines, Thonet's world-famous bentwood chairs are enduring classics. They're made of steam-bent beechwood, and their construction appears to surpass the natural possibilities of the material. The chairs' unique blend of grace and strength enables them to complement everything from stately, Victorian parlors to modern, sun-drenched lofts with style and ease.

### CLASSIC, ONCE AGAIN

Gebruder Thonet has been steaming and bending wood for more than a century, and it is no fluke that classics such as the Prague and Tivoli chairs have remained in continuous production ever since. These chairs were well ahead of their time: Their simplified form hinted at things to come and has widely influenced chair design ever since.

These chairs are at once modern and antique. Their open, airy profile and cane seat and back make them a natural choice, whether for a handsome villa on a tropical isle or a modern, sunny breakfast nook in the Arizona desert.

### STURDY, STYLISH, AND ADAPTABLE

For more than a century, Thonet's chairs have offered timeless style and exceptional versatility. Although they're delicate in appearance, bentwood chairs are actually quite stable and strong, making them ideal for everyday use in a breakfast or dining room.

While some of the chairs are characterized by exuberant, elaborately curved frames, other models appear quite simple and restrained. Some feature upholstered seats and backs, while others use caning or a combination of both. Such details significantly change the look of the piece, alternatively adding mass or transparency to the essentially fluid silhouette. In addition, many of the designs are available with or without arms. Because of their relatively diminutive scale, the versions without arms are useful as extra seating around a dining table. At the same time, bentwood armchairs are good multipurpose pieces that can have a place in a bedroom, study, or living room.

## SUBTLE CURVES

A set of Prague arm- and side chairs surround a simple chrome-legged, wood-topped dining table in this modern dining area. The subtle curves of Thonet's chairs are echoed by the chrome tubing of the furnishings in the adjoining sitting area, a simple but elegant juxtaposition in this spare, modern space.

## ELEGANT LINES

The light woods and elegant lines of Thonet's Tivoli open-back chair provide a fluid contrast in a dining area defined by strong horizontal lines. Paired with a dark stained wood table, the natural beechwood chairs lend a light touch to a room.

# A Modern Icon

The elegant, understated Barcelona chair is one of the most original and renowned furniture designs of the twentieth century. A pair of simple, welded steel cross members, polished to a smooth finish, make up the chair's sculptural frame, while wide, leather straps support tufted seat and back cushions. The timeless creation of Ludwig Mies van der Rohe, the Barcelona chair is distilled to the point of perfection and is as fresh as any contemporary design.

## ARCHITECTURAL
The graceful profile of Mies van der Rohe's Barcelona chair exemplifies the architectural influence in modern design. The supple, tufted-leather cushions are a common element of van der Rohe's designs.

DIMENSIONS: W 30 IN. (75 CM) x D 30 IN. (76 CM); 17 IN. (43 CM); SEAT

## WHAT MAKES IT CLASSIC

- *VERSATILITY: Used side by side, Barcelona chairs can substitute for a sofa. Their pronounced, slanted back and seat offer cradle-like comfort. When paired with the matching ottoman, they offer all the satisfaction of a reclining chair and all the style and drama of a modern masterpiece.*

- *FIT FOR ROYALTY: The original chairs were designed for the king and queen of Spain's official visit to the Deutscher Werkbund Pavilion at the 1929 World Exposition in Barcelona and were upholstered in white kidskin. It has been said that this elegant chair is indeed a modern throne.*

- *ARCHITECTURAL INSPIRATION: The tufted grid of the chair's upholstery detail is generally attributed to van der Rohe's collaborator, Lilly Reich. The pattern is said to have derived from the Deutscher Werkbund Pavilion's gridded plan, which explains why this chair works well in strong architectural spaces.*

## INTERNATIONAL STYLE
Although its creator is associated with the strict functionalism of the International Style, the Barcelona chair is not at all severe. One of the most beautiful of modern chair designs, this sculptural piece reflects its creator's keen sense of proportion, craftsmanship, and restraint. These precise attributes make the Barcelona chair a favorite among architects and designers.

The fluid, graceful lines of the Barcelona chair both complement contemporary interiors and provide a modern counterpoint to traditional antiques. Purists prefer classic black or brown leather upholstery for sleek, minimal rooms, while others use playful, irreverent alternatives, such as brightly colored patent leather, for more eclectic environments. An extremely versatile piece, the armless lounge chair can be positioned anywhere in a room.

## CHAIR, REVISITED
The Barcelona chair redefines itself in response to its surroundings. While the chair often is grouped in pairs, as it was in the original Barcelona Pavilion, a single piece can serve as a dramatic gesture in a small space. Van der Rohe also designed a Barcelona ottoman and coffee table for those who desire a complete ensemble, a stylish choice for a modern, architectural space. Pair it with contrasting textures and forms—natural fibers, Asian-influenced antique tables, or even an overstuffed, contemporary sofa—to make it the centerpiece of a dramatically designed room.

< GRACEFUL
Ludwig Mies van der Rohe's Barcelona chair and loveseat add lush, comfortable seating to this spare, modern setting. While the shape of the chair's cushions echo the right angles of the tile walls and floor, its gracefully shaped legs and soft, tufted-leather seats provide a gentle contrast to the harsh geometry of the room.

# An Elegant Expression

**DECO**

Inspired by forties French deco styling, with a nod to earlier French influences, Barbara Barry's Oval X-Back dining room chair combines classical forms with modern minimalism.

DIMENSIONS: W 27 IN. (69 CM) x H 38 IN. (97 CM), x D 24 IN. (61 CM)

**WHAT MAKES IT CLASSIC**

- *BEYOND ECLECTIC: By blending modern and classical influences, the Oval X-Back chair speaks to many styles and eras. It adds a hint of history to a modern space just as easily as it fits in with antiques.*

- *VERSATILITY IN FORM: Upholstery dramatically changes the look of this chair and allows it to work within many decorative schemes. A smaller-scale version of the Oval X-Back chair provides comfortable and commodious seating around a dining table.*

- *STYLE BY DESIGN: Los Angeles—based designer Barbara Barry is known for harmonious interiors that embody a relaxed, modern, and distinctly West Coast sensibility. Barry favors subtle, tonal palettes with clean lines and sensual textures, all of which inform her stunning chair design.*

Sleek and lithe, Barbara Barry's Oval X-Back chair provides a refreshing, contemporary twist to traditional French formality. Characterized by clean lines and proportions, this updated piece has an upholstered seat and back with rounded wooden arms and graceful, slightly curved legs. Its elegance and refinement evoke Barry's signature finesse and impeccable style.

**A MODERN TAKE ON A TRADITIONAL SHAPE**

The Oval X-Back chair can dress up any room with its linear silhouette and tailored upholstery. A reverential nod to numerous historical styles, this piece offers an elegant alternative to a Louis XVI chair or a contemporary stand-in for a French deco design. Yet, while this chair derives its classic shape from historical precedents, its updated proportions and details give it a fresh, modern appeal.

A timeless piece that defines eclecticism, this chair can be transformed according to the upholstery material with which it is paired. Sumptuous silk or delicate leather complements its lithe frame, while a vibrant pattern accentuates the chair's inherent geometry. The back and seat can be covered in contrasting colors for a playful, two-tone look.

> STUNNING

With their elegant form and deep, java finish, Barbara Barry's Oval X-Back chairs are stunning on their own. But pair them with her signature dining table, and you've created a formal setting that is at once classical and totally modern.

# Totally Tubular

**TUBE FRAME**
Bicycle handlebars are said to have been the inspiration for the Cesca chair's signature metal-tube frame.

DIMENSIONS: W 24 IN. (61 CM) X D 24 IN. (60 CM) X H 31 IN. (80 CM)

## WHAT MAKES IT CLASSIC

- *SOFT YET HARD: Softened by its wood frame and caned seat and back, the Cesca chair is a logical choice for those who want a modern look without hard edges. Its playful blend of natural and high-tech materials give it a modern edge without rendering it sterile or cold.*

- *TIMELESS PRESENCE: With its sophisticated profile, unusual mix of materials, and universal appeal, the Cesca chair is a hard design to pin down in terms of a stylistic era. The chair looks as fresh today as it did when it was first designed three-quarters of a century ago.*

- *ORIGINS: Architect Marcel Breuer generally is considered the first to create a tubular steel, cantilever chair. This chair was named after his daughter, Francesca.*

< INVITING
In this sunny kitchen, a set of charming Cesca chairs provides ample seating without taking up lots of space. Breuer's unique design makes the chairs seem to float above the floor, and the cane seats allow the light to filter through. The result is an inviting dinette that manages to fill the space without interrupting its airy, open feel.

With its S-shaped, cantilevered frame, the Cesca chair appears to defy gravity. Designed in 1925 by Marcel Breuer, the Cesca chair is a tubular steel cantilever armchair with a caned seat and a back framed in bentwood. It is a descendant of traditional bentwood furniture and reportedly inspired by the curved, tubular steel handlebars of a bicycle. Breuer conceived this chair to furnish the rooms of the modern age. A radical departure from the heavy, upholstered furniture favored during the Victorian era, this chair was designed as a practical and "hygienic" alternative to its predecessors.

## COOL BUT NOT COLD

While the Cesca chair's thin, tubular supports and delicate caning seem light and airy, this is a remarkably sturdy piece that can withstand heavy use. Because it is both comfortable and resilient, the chair is a practical yet stylish choice for either a breakfast or dining room. The Cesca chair's combination of metal, wood, and caning make it a versatile piece that complements many different table styles. A glass-topped table, for example, accentuates the chair's geometric cane patterning, while intensely colored table linens set up a study in contrasts. Lightweight, functional, and handsome, the Cesca chair is an ever-popular design that is distinctly modern yet comfortable and warm.

# Join the Club

**COZY**

Tailored, boxy, and, above all, comfortable, a club chair is the quintessential cozy spot, perfect for reading or just relaxing. This example, designed by Jean-Michel Frank, is upholstered in wool felt.

DIMENSIONS: VARY

### WHAT MAKES IT CLASSIC

- *THE BEST SEAT IN THE HOUSE: Popularized during the twenties, the club chair is a timeless lounge piece. Pair it with a matching ottoman, a stunning lamp, and a rich, substantial side table for the ultimate reading nook.*

- *AN INVESTMENT IN STYLE AND SUBSTANCE: Supple, leather upholstery gives the chair a sleek look that is at the same time warm and inviting. The chair's appearance actually improves as the leather ages. Look for models with high, supportive backs and low, pitched seats. The armrests should be generously scaled with a slight incline.*

- *THE CORNERSTONE OF A ROOM: In a room defined by hard edges—perhaps one with lots of leggy tables, wood-framed mission furniture, or more delicate modern pieces— the heft and soft bulk of a fine club chair provide a sense of substance.*

Generally associated with the twenties and thirties, the club chair is a classic lounge piece characterized by a low, pitched seat, high back, and rounded, bolster arms. Fully upholstered, usually in leather, with discreet wooden feet, it is the chair for which everyone fights. Numerous contemporary designers have updated this popular style by adding new details or altering its lines and proportions ever so slightly. But no one has dared to disturb its chic, clean profile and comfortable scale.

### COMFORT AND CHARACTER

Designed to embrace and support the sitter, the club chair is both elegant and inviting. A pair of club chairs adds a relaxed, masculine presence to a living room and works well with other solid, straight-edged pieces. Used with an ottoman and positioned in a secluded, well-lit corner, this chair is ideal for relaxing, reading, or watching television. Many designers offer a contemporary take on this classic style that has an angular, deco-inspired aesthetic. Sleek, updated versions are at home in contemporary interiors that need softening; But their balanced proportions and classic style are compatible with more traditional pieces, too.

∧ LUSH

Two pillow-backed club chairs straddle a charming side table, making this sunny spot a perfect location for conversation or an after-supper cocktail. In pairs, club chairs—with their substantial proportions and lush upholstery—can have all the impact of a larger sofa.

∧ WILLOWY

With its willowy profile and comfortable seat, the Windsor chair works beautifully as additional seating in a living room or sun room. Its high back gives it a sense of substance without disrupting the flow of traffic or natural light, the way that a larger, upholstered chair would.

< UNMISTAKABLE

A blend of modern sparseness and traditional details, this stunning white dining room is brought to life by the addition of a vintage farm table surrounded by a set of antique Windsor chairs. The dark wood tones of the chairs provide a striking contrast with the white walls and natural wood floor; the repetition of their tall, arched backs makes them the unmistakable focal point of the room.

# A Classic through the Centuries

Dating from the seventeenth century, the Windsor chair integrates pieces of bentwood in its graceful, curved frame. Its distinctive back appears in a variety of forms, but it is the angular fan and rounded loop shapes that are the best-known and most popular today. Other features include a comfortable, slightly contoured seat and slender, turned legs that are set at a pronounced angle. The result is a remarkably strong structure with a minimum of material and weight—a design that will never go out of date.

## INTO THE WOODS

The Windsor's thin, hardwood turnings and elegant curves make this chair a tasteful addition to any room. While this piece is clearly at home with other early-American or English antiques, the Windsor chair's simple, linear silhouette also complements transitional settings. With its carved seat and high back shaped for comfort, the Windsor is a practical, versatile piece that works well in a breakfast or dining room but can also be used in a sitting or living room.

The chair's uncluttered design spans the centuries with uncompromised style and grace. A suite of Windsor arm- and side chairs can surround an antique farm table in one home as well as it can a sleek, steel-topped dinette in another. The design goes from desk chair, to dining chair, to porch rocker and manages to suit each situation as though it were designed for that very purpose.

The Windsor chair's distinctive shape has inspired numerous twentieth-century chair designs. Danish designer Hans Wegner based his 1947 Peacock chair, a favorite among modern collectors, on this historic English precedent. An updated version of the Windsor is a desirable choice for a contemporary scheme.

## STUNNING FORM

With its high, curved back, detailed with a fan of graceful stretchers, the classic Windsor side chair may be the perfect dining chair. This stunning form works in settings ranging from formal period dining rooms to eclectic modern spaces.

DIMENSIONS: W 21 IN. (53 CM) X H 41 IN. (104 CM) IS AVERAGE

## WHAT MAKES IT CLASSIC

- *FINE MATERIALS AND CRAFTSMANSHIP: Early examples of Windsor chairs incorporate different varieties of wood in a single piece, such as a sturdy combination of maple and hickory. These marvels of the joiner's craft are highly sought after by collectors.*

- *ACCESSIBLE ANTIQUES: While authentic, period Windsor chairs command high prices, extremely accurate reproductions are widely available in a variety of hardwoods and finishes. Some manufacturers offer distressed finishes to imitate the effects of age and wear.*

- *HISTORIC PRECEDENTS: Developed in England, the Windsor chair became popular in America during the eighteenth century and has remained so ever since. George Washington is said to have purchased twenty-four Windsors in 1796 for use at Mount Vernon.*

# The Essence of Postwar Modernism

## BIOMORPHIC SCULPTURE
Designed by Charles and Ray Eames in 1946, and produced by Herman Miller, the molded-plywood dining chair is an icon of midcentury modernism. The chair combines its creators' early interest in abstract, biomorphic sculpture with their quest for efficient, practical, and accessible modern furniture.

DIMENSIONS: H 30 IN. (75 CM) X D 20 IN. (52 CM) X W 20 IN. (52 CM)

## WHAT MAKES IT CLASSIC

- *BASIC VERSATILITY: The almost puritan simplicity of the Eames chair belies its complex character. This is a chair that can take center stage in a minimalistic atmosphere or become an integral but unobtrusive component of a more eclectic interior.*

- *ERGONOMIC ARTISTRY: Produced from minimal materials, the chair is renowned for its comfort, stability, and resilience.*

- *INNOVATIVE DESIGN: The result of tireless experimentation with wood-molding techniques that the Eameses developed for the manufacturing of aircraft parts and leg splints for the military, these radically simple designs, according to the* Washington Post, *"changed the way that America sat down."*

Contrasting broad planes of wood with sinewy chrome, the Eames plywood chair (named in military fashion DCM) is a lesson in the economics of design. Stripped down to its essence, the chair emerges as a judicious juxtaposition of seat, back, and legs that is at once substantial and ethereal.

What is perhaps most striking about the Eames plywood chair is that despite its appearance, it is an extremely comfortable chair. Gently contoured and carefully pitched, the DCM is one of the few modern wooden chairs that provide comfortable seating for extended periods of time. Made of five-ply plywood, the chair's seat and backrest express the body's curves, while its chromed steel, tubular legs, and back brace assume a graphic, skeletal form.

## SIMPLICITY REVISED
Different finishes enable the functional, clean-lined DCM to assume versatile roles in a given decorative program. Natural wood provides casual warmth, while ebony creates a more sleek and sophisticated appearance. Although this piece, along with its companion lounge chair (LCM), are closely associated with the postwar aesthetic, the DCM's spare, elegant profile can be an inspired addition to a more traditional interior, as well. Consider, for example, the Eames chair as an unexpected part of a Shaker-inspired interior: the chair's geometric simplicity perfectly complements the humble atmosphere, while adding a refreshing breath of modern, sculptural beauty to the scene.

> SINEWY
The curvaceous, molded plywood seats of Charles and Ray Eames' charming chair provide a natural foil for its sinewy metal legs. Paired with a simple table, the chairs create an elegant yet utterly practical dining suite that is pleasing but never stuffy.

# classic lounging

Free-Form Serpentine Sofa

Eames Sofa Compact

Shabby Chic Sofa

Stickley Settle

Mies van der Rohe Sofa

Le Corbusier Grand Confort Sofa

Florence Knoll Sofa

Sectional Sofa

Nest Sofa

Camelback Sofa

# Simplifying a Space

**SUBSTANTIAL**
Kagan's sofa is meant to simplify a room. Substantial in size and shape, it can serve as the only piece of furniture in even a large, open space.

DIMENSIONS: VARY

## WHAT MAKES IT CLASSIC

- *CONVERSATION PIECE: Kagan's Serpentine sofa is multidirectional—sitters can face any number of ways. This arrangement creates intimate spaces within larger areas, a perfect way to cozy up a vast space such as a loft or great room.*

- *CUSTOM CLASSIC: Each Serpentine sofa was unique—Kagan would visit a home to determine the best place for the sofa, and what size it should be. The designer still works the same way, although standard sizes are also available.*

- *INFLUENTIAL DESIGN: Long before many furniture designers began to embrace Kagan's aesthetic, sweeping curves and organic shapes became de rigueur in other areas of design—the kidney-shaped swimming pool and the exuberant patterns of fifties china, for example, were products of the biomorphic look Kagan (along with Isamu Noguchi and a few others) pioneered.*

When you need a dynamic sofa that at once fills a room and defines an area for conversation without challenging the openness of a modern home, consider Vladimir Kagan's Free-Form Serpentine sofa. The broad planes, sweeping spaces, and open plans that typify so much modern architecture benefit from the sexy curves and unexpected geometry of Kagan's classic. Intended to simplify a large space by reducing the amount of furniture in it, the Serpentine sofa offers plenty of seating and lots of visual impact in a single piece.

## CLASSIC TWIST

This sweeping, serpentine sofa might have seemed outlandish when it debuted in 1949, but Kagan insists that he was simply responding to his clients' needs. "They collected huge paintings—Pollock, Rothko, Hans Hoffman—that needed the whole wall," he explained. "I designed a sofa that could float in the room. We could liberate the walls and focus on the whole artwork." Kagan's theory continues to ring true today: the twists and turns of this chic yet utterly functional sofa work well in today's open home plans, pulling furnishings away from the walls and creating definitive "rooms" within vast spaces.

Consider the way this curvaceous couch can divide a combination living and dining area, for example. The low profile doesn't interrupt the open feel by blocking natural light, while the free-form shape creates a definitive room divider without appearing rigid or awkward

While Kagan's furniture was decidedly new, he relied on both traditional and recent materials. The base of the Serpentine sofa was carved from solid walnut, and the entire piece was finished in custom fabric. A new wonder material, foam rubber, allowed Kagan to go where no designer had gone before and make a comfortable sofa without loose cushions. Down and horsehair complemented the foam to create a soft but tight one-piece cushion.

< SERPENTINE
True to the intentions of its creator, the serpentine sofa works as the only piece of furniture in this stunning architectural space. Its rich red color and fluid form creates a bold statement, yet the sofa remains true to its functional purpose, providing ample seating around the fireplace.

# Built for Comfort and Style

**SPIRITED**

Charles and Ray Eames are known for playful and inspired furniture and architecture that was infused with the fresh spirit of their time. Their tiny Sofa Compact offers all the impact and seating of a larger sofa in half the space of many traditional sofas.

DIMENSIONS: H 35 IN. (89 CM) x D 30 IN. (76.2 CM) x L 72 IN. (184 CM)

**WHAT MAKES IT CLASSIC**

- *ACCESSIBLE STYLE: The Eameses used innovative techniques and materials to create furniture that was durable and beautiful and, because it could be mass-produced, affordable. The original model of this sofa was meant for offices and sported vinyl upholstery. Today, Herman Miller has foregone the vinyl and offers versions in seven colors of fabric, of which the most popular shade is bright red.*

- *HISTORICAL ORIGINS: The late forties and early fifties, when the Eameses created their best-known designs, was an era flush with innovative materials, optimism, and a great desire among consumers to try everything they had missed during the Depression and World War II—the newer the better.*

Small but stately, the Eames Sofa Compact is the couch distilled to its very essence. Designed in 1954 by Charles and Ray Eames, this sofa is a marvel of minimal engineering. A simple, steel structure cradles three long, upholstered cushions, all of which sit on twinned, chromed steel bases. The design is svelte, striking, and compact.

The Eames Sofa Compact began as a built-in for the innovative Los Angeles house that the Eameses designed in the late forties. It worked out so well that they developed a freestanding version, first in wire and later in the present, steel-supported version. Their design bears little resemblance to most sofas. Whereas most lounge seating is plush, massive, and heavy, the Sofa Compact's profile is thin and distinctive and its structure surprisingly simple. Yet this minimal sofa does much more than save space. Its urethane foam cushions offer firm support, while the curved, sectioned back gently cradles you when you sit.

**THE LITTLE COUCH THAT THINKS BIG**

As its name implies, the Sofa Compact is perfect for spaces that are too small for a traditional couch: an alcove, a sewing room, a wide hallway. It manages to fit into tiny living rooms without throwing the space off balance, and works beautifully as additional guest seating in a home office. Yet it is also the perfect sofa for a larger space that is defined by modern forms and has an open, airy feel.

Although the Sofa Compact has an unusual design, it is appropriate for a wide variety of interiors. At one end of the spectrum, it's perfect for the retro, space age look revived by magazines recently, especially when it's paired with some of the more exuberant lamps, chairs, and accessories created in the sixties. At the other end, the sofa's grace, simplicity, and beauty—so typical of the Eameses' spartan modernism—enable it to serve as the centerpiece in a room of classic, midcentury furniture, especially other Eames creations such as their wood and metal lounge chairs or their molded, rosewood chair and ottoman.

∧ AESTHETIC PUNCH
With its sweeping cathedral ceiling, two stories of windows, and wide-open plan, the tiny Sofa Compact might seem like an odd choice for this large space. But laden with rich fabrics and opulent pillows, the Eames simplified sofa is anything but minimalist and packs all of the aesthetic punch of a larger piece.

∧ FOUNDATION
Slipcovered in vintage fabrics and laden with
lots of soft, overstuffed pillows, a simple and
comfy couch provides the focal point for this
charming sitting room. A study in white, the
faded florals, whitewashed tables, and antique
accessories show off the foundations of the
Shabby Chic aesthetic.

# The Comforts of Home

**OVERSTUFFED**

Shabby Chic introduced practical to pretty with this simple, soft sofa. Overstuffed and slipcovered in fabrics that are easy to care for, the Shabby Chic sofa made white—bright white, creamy white, antique white—user friendly for the first time.

DIMENSIONS: VARY

## WHAT MAKES IT CLASSIC

- *SLIPCOVERED SIMPLICITY: The slipcovers that now stands as a kind of shorthand for Shabby Chic began out of necessity—Rachel Aswell needed to protect her own furniture from her two young children. Those slipcovers seemed to evoke the moneyed ease of a summer in the Hamptons or the English countryside, and they spawned a whole approach to fabrics and accessories.*

- *FROM PRACTICAL TO PRACTICALLY OPULENT: While Aswell chose resilient, washable white denim for her first coverings, high-style Shabby Chic now relies on fancier and softer fabrics. A bright white cotton is still the standard covering for this classic sofa, but patterned and textured materials, including matelassé and chenille, are attractive variations.*

- *AN ENTIRE VISION: Shabby Chic is a style that revels in coziness, comfort, originality, and the pleasures of a naturally evolving interior. The style's founder calls it a shunning of the too new, modern, or ostentatious and a rebellion against perfection.*

The big, cushy, slipcovered Shabby Chic sofa insists that a living room should be lived in, that it should be the center of a home. It's a sofa that calls out, "Sit on me." And it's a sofa that represents an entire way of life.

The Shabby Chic look starts with the sofa and easily radiates into the rest of the home. Pairing the comfy sofa with gently faded antiques, a floral arrangement or two, mixed fabrics and textures creates, as the pioneer of Shabby, Rachel Aswell puts it, "the cozy familiarity of a well-worn pair of faded blue jeans."

The Shabby Chic aesthetic works well with timeworn, classic interiors—rooms with lots of old moldings, stunning windows, and distressed plaster walls blend perfectly with the kind of gently old-fashioned style that Aswell promotes. Yet the faded fabrics and overstuffed comfort of the Shabby Chic line also work extremely well with modern, less ornamented spaces, primarily because they lend a sense of warmth and history to newer construction.

## VARIATIONS ON THE THEME OF COMFORT

There are a few formal variations on the Shabby Chic sofa. There is a curvy, classic version with scrolled arms, a tighter, more formal one with straight arms, and a contemporary, less cushy variation, among others. They all share the comfortable, overstuffed quality that defines the Shabby Chic aesthetic. The stuffing usually comprises feathers or down around a foam core, so sitters can sink deeply into cushions that conform to their bodies. Size is important: These are big sofas that obey the rules of classic proportions and let people curl up into the corners.

Very often a plethora of pillows, including overstuffed ones that match and small and large throw pillows in subtly contrasting patterns, complement a Shabby Chic sofa. The preference for subtle in the pillows extends to the entire Shabby Chic home, where a mix of new and old, fancy and folksy prevails.

# Stunning Design Made Functional

**FAMILY FRIENDLY**
Gustav Stickley's settles—at first, fairly simple, upholstered benches with wooden arms—were designed for rooms that were to be lived in. Beautiful and functional, these oak forms offered family-friendly practicality for rooms "where children grow and thrive."

DIMENSIONS: L 68 IN. (173 CM) x W 36 IN. (91 CM) x D 29 IN. (74 CM)

**WHAT MAKES IT CLASSIC**

- *INTEGRITY IN FURNITURE: Influenced as much by the English Arts and Crafts movement as by the simple beauty and craftsmanship of American Shaker furniture, Stickley set out to create a new aesthetic that expanded on an uncluttered look and incorporated fine, natural materials and master craftsmanship.*

- *A TRULY AMERICAN STYLE: Today, the Mission style is often associated with the West, but Stickley's Craftsman studio was in upstate New York, and the advances in architecture during his time—the Prairie School as well as the bungalow craze—began in the East and Midwest.*

- *A NEW VISION: When he began designing at the turn of the century, the typical middle- or upper-class home was a riot of patterns and furniture. Stickley described the prevailing style: "a stuffy, formal parlor is crowded with fussy furniture ... and bric-a-brac." His own approach eschewed the clutter of the parlor for the, more open and casual "living room."*

If you're looking for furnishings that are simple, livable, and practical yet also outstanding examples of fine craftsmanship and inspired design, you need not look much further than the classic designs of Gustav Stickley. With their simple, geometric forms and natural materials, these stunning sofas are at once rustic and modern, spare yet quietly inviting.

Stickley's classic settles embrace his own ideal of spare yet comfortable furnishings, and inspired the design aesthetic more commonly known as Mission style. The designer's furniture company offered several variations of the settle, among them the slat-back version, which is the most recognizable as Mission style; the Prairie settle, which had solid arms and back and wraparound upholstered cushions; and the spindle settle, notable for its more delicate slats. The Prairie model is the most horizontal and sleek, exhibiting the influence of the architecture coming into fashion in the early 1900s.

**VISION AND VERSATILITY**
In any versions—old or new, slatted or Prairie—Stickley's core design beliefs influence the settle. His furniture, he wrote, upholds "the ideas of honesty of materials, solidity of construction, utility, adaptability to place, and aesthetic effect." Ornament was forbidden (he called it "a parasite"), and materials, especially American white oak, were allowed to speak for themselves.

The basic design of Stickley's settles lends itself to a variety of different interiors. A change in the fabric allows for surprising variations on the form. The original settle came with a spring-seat cushion upholstered in leather, velour, velvet, or Craftsman canvas. Pillows—Stickley offered sheepskin versions—were an extra eight dollars each. The Stickley settles currently produced bow to modern conventions and feature a solid wall of deep, comfortable cushions against which to relax, either in dark leather or a soft fabric in the muted, darker tones idealized by bungalow architects and interior decorators.

∧ CENTER STAGE
Usually associated with Arts and Crafts architecture or southwestern-theme décors, the simple style of Stickley's mission furniture can work equally well in more Spartan, modern interiors as well. Here, the rich oak finish of Stickley sofa, chair, and other furnishings take center stage against pale white walls and light oak floors.

∧ HARMONIOUS HORIZONTAL
In this spare but sweeping modern interior,
Mies van der Rohe's minimalist sofa creates a
perfect spot to lounge and take in the stunning
view. With no bulky backboard and only one
bolster, this simple daybed does not disrupt the
harmonious horizontal lines that define the space.

# Less is More

**BOLDLY MINIMALIST**

Pared down to its elemental purpose, the van der Rohe sofa is a lounge piece that lies somewhere between a daybed and a sofa. The tufted, leather cushions and rich, rosewood frame lend a sense of warmth to the boldly minimalist piece.

DIMENSIONS: H 24 IN. (62 CM) X D 38 IN. (97 CM) X L 78 IN. (198 CM)

---

**WHAT MAKES IT CLASSIC**

- *MINIMALISM DEFINED: Inspired by classical designs, van der Rohe tried to strip down his furniture to the purest basics of form, proportion, and material. This stunning example of his mission serves as distinctive, comfortable seating and represents the most spare yet beautiful impulses of early thirties modernism.*

- *SOFA METAMORPHOSIS: Designed in 1930, van der Rohe's sofa has withstood the test of time with only minor alterations. Current models utilize stainless steel rather than chromed steel, and the piece is more commonly used as secondary, lounge seating or as a daybed.*

- *A SECRET HISTORY: This sophisticated piece shares some of the warmest traits of van der Rohe's Barcelona chair, including its tufted leather cushion. The chair and sofa complement each other so well that many people assume they were both designed for van der Rohe's landmark 1929 Barcelona Pavilion; in fact, the sofa was made for Philip Johnson's New York City apartment and didn't receive its public premiere until 1931, in Berlin.*

Ludwig Mies van der Rohe is often credited with coining the minimalist dictum "less is more," though the saying predated the architect by several decades. More appropriate to the stunningly simple and beautiful sofa van der Rohe designed in 1930 was a phrase the architect and designer often used to describe his work: "almost nothing." This eminently spare sofa might speak to its designer's minimalist sensibilities, but it is not spartan. Composed of rich materials, it boasts a profile that is elegant yet thoroughly modern.

Comprising rich rosewood, supple leather, and polished, chromed steel, the backless sofa is an essay in the luxury of fine materials. Stripped down to the barest of essentials, the sofa still offers comfort with generous proportions: It measures 2 meters long and 1 meter deep and has a leather bolster running along one side.

**RETHINKING THE SOFA**

Even if it's made with the softest leather and most well-tended rosewood, this sofa can sometimes seem a bit severe. For his own interiors, van der Rohe often coupled the sofa with a pair of Barcelona chairs and ottomans to create a semiformal interaction of furniture. Elsewhere, the unusual design and simple form of van der Rohe's classic piece invite improvisational arrangements. The backless, one-bolster design and deep proportions of the couch encourage pulling it away from the walls so that it can be approached for seating on three sides.

# Equipped for Living

Luxurious and comfortable, yet defined by cool, hard edges, Le Corbusier's Grand Confort sofa is a lesson in contrasts. A stack of stuffed, leather cushions encased in a tubular steel frame, this stunning design offers the inviting luxury of an overstuffed couch with the chic symmetry of the most modern, austere furnishings.

French architect and designer Le Corbusier famously proclaimed that modern houses were "machines for living in" and called the furniture he designed to be used in them "equipment." Fortunately, Le Corbusier's ideas about living included comfort as well as function. The Grand Confort sofa—designed in two- and three-seat versions—and chair provide not only a sense of "sculpture in space," but also a deep, lush, and comfortable place to sit.

The Grand Confort sofa and chair challenged traditional ideas of how luxurious furniture could be made and how it should look. Le Corbusier combined the idea of a club chair, with its thick leather cushions and some basic principles of modernism, such as the use of rigorous geometry, new, industrial materials, and an exposed structure. The result was one of the most striking creations of the machine age: an almost perfect cube of highly polished chrome tubes that cradles oversized, black leather cushions.

## MODERNISM THAT WORKS
Consider pairing this classic piece with the matching love seat or club chair for a unified and balanced grouping. The simple profile and welcoming materials of Le Corbusier's sofa and chairs make them suitable for almost any modern interior. The stark yet rich materials add warmth to a space without overpowering it and blend gracefully with both organic and modern materials. The black leather and chrome are grounded by a gleaming, hardwood floor and strike stunning silhouettes against pure white walls. For extra impact, add color to the room, be it a solid wall of vibrant red paint or a soft palette of neutrals.

## STUDY IN CONSTRASTS
Gleaming chrome meets warm, supple leather in Le Corbusier's Grand Confort sofa. By pairing hard edges with soft cushions, this sofa combines a modern aesthetic and old-fashioned comfort.

DIMENSIONS: H 27 IN. (69.8 CM) x D 26 IN. (66 CM) x W 66 IN. (167.6 CM)

## WHAT MAKES IT CLASSIC

- *REAL-LIFE DESIGN: While a great many modern designs offer comfort and practicality, the Grand Confort delivers above and beyond. Soft and supple enough for serious lounging, the precisely fitted cushions stay neatly in place, yet they can easily be removed for cleaning.*

- *A STUDY IN CONTRASTS: The mathematically precise shape of Le Corbusier's sofa, combined with the cool lines formed by the tubular chrome frame, create a stunning, precise, and interesting juxtaposition of textures, shapes, and materials. At once dark and bright, soft and hard, cool and comfortable, the Grand Confort sofa is a wonderful blend of sleek, modern lines and voluptuous luxury.*

- *MODERNISM TIMES TWO: The Grand Confort—an example of the fresh, bold modernism of the late twenties—was reintroduced in the sixties and quickly became an icon of the new International Style. By the end of the sixties, the Grand Confort had become a familiar sight in both the offices and living rooms.*

< LUXURIOUS
Artfully arranged, a suite of Le Corbusier furniture
completes a modern take on a traditional living
room. Designed for comfort, these luxurious
leather-and-chrome furnishings create a firm
foundation for room's expansive design.

∧ WEIGHTLESSNESS
With its upholstered, boxy cushions and industrial metal base, the Florence Knoll sofa combines traditional form with a splash of modern
edginess. The slender, minimalist legs lend a
sense of weightlessness to the otherwise
substantial sofa, making it a perfect choice for a
spartan interior like this one. The marble-topped
side table echoes the sofa's unique styling.

# A Rigorous Beauty

### STYLED FOR OPEN SPACE

Florence Knoll designed her signature line to suit the vast, open spaces that were coming into fashion in the late fifties. "The interior decorators of the time had no knowledge of modern architecture," Knoll said. "Or, if they had, they were generally out of sympathy with it."

DIMENSIONS: W 90.5 IN. (230 CM) x D 31.5 IN. (80 CM) x H 31.5 IN. (80 CM)

---

### WHAT MAKES IT CLASSIC

- *AT HOME IN ANY SPACE: Designed for the airy, open spaces of the new architecture and interiors then coming into fashion, the spare profile of Knoll's sofa provides an island of calm repose without interrupting the clean, expansive feel of the room. Yet this simple sofa also works great as seating in small spaces where more substantial or complicated forms might be aesthetic distractions.*

- *SIMPLICITY IN PROFILE: With its clean lines, precise design, and forceful, solid colors, Knoll's line offers minimalist style in a profile that is still familiar and comfortable. First designed for offices, Knoll's sofa (and the scores of imitations it spawned) migrated quickly to the home, along with the work of some of her contemporaries, notably Charles and Ray Eames.*

- *COMPLETE VISION: As part of the Knoll Planning Unit in the fifties and sixties, Florence Knoll's job was to design complete, "organic" interiors that synthesized space, furniture, color, fabric, and other details. Few of the era's progressive furniture designers had bothered to make couches, which Knoll saw as an opportunity.*

Stripped down, almost elemental in form, Florence Knoll's sofa is a lesson in symmetry and restraint. Three equal, forcefully geometric sections form a sofa-sized rectangle; arms and back rise perfectly straight from the base. The three pairs of thin, square-sectioned, chromed steel tubing that support the sofa easily go unnoticed. As a result, the piece seems to float 6 inches above the ground. This spare and subdued design is as fresh and modern today as it was when it was introduced fifty years ago.

The key part to a suite of lounge seating that Knoll designed in 1954, the sofa is long, rectangular, and closer to the ground than the average piece of furniture. This emphatically horizontal line of Knoll's design reflected the new casualness of offices and living rooms: People were no longer expected to sit ramrod straight as they entertained. The lower elevation of lounge seating also directed the sitter's attention to the coffee table. The entire effect was sleek, long, and clean.

### A CLASSIC THAT ANCHORS A ROOM

Today, the Knoll look, and this sofa in particular, is a sort of shorthand for the optimistic, pure modernism of the fifties. Grouped with a matching Knoll side table or other midcentury classics—such as the Eameses' "surfboard" coffee table or George Nelson's slatted bench—this sofa can anchor a re-creation of the clean, easy, modern living of that era. Alternatively, grouped with later Scandinavian bookshelves, tables, and other furnishings, the sofa is easily updated for a fresh, contemporary look.

# Making the Most of a Space

**CALM COMFORT**

This simple but elegant sectional sofa by Piero Lissoni for Cassina creates ample seating with the calm comfort of a singular unit of furniture. Paired with a matching double ottoman and a trio of elegant occasional tables, it becomes the central conversation spot for parties.

DIMENSIONS: VARY

## WHAT MAKES IT CLASSIC

- *A PLACE FOR EVERYONE TO SIT: Sectional sofas are quite large and make use of every inch of floor space they cover. Providing ample seating in a conversation-friendly arrangement, they are the perfect sofas for spaces that are often used for entertaining.*

- *FAMILY-FRIENDLY DESIGN: With room for everyone to sit and watch TV or gather around a game board or picture book, these sofas easily become the hub of household activities.*

- *A DESIGNER PEDIGREE: Although the sectional is often identified with the modular craze of the late sixties, it was, in fact, a product of the thirties, pioneered by the innovative designer Gilbert Rohde, who worked for Herman Miller, and by Russel Wright.*

Offering lots of seats and a form that immediately makes an impression, the sectional sofa is the piece of furniture that makes chairs and loveseats nervous. Indeed, why opt for three or four pieces of furniture when a single piece (or perhaps a group disguised as a single unit) can do so much, so well? While a great many mass-marketed sectional sofas cater to the basement television-room aesthetic, the form is actually rooted in early thirties modern design, and a number of stunning, stylish models are available from top design houses.

## SEATING SOLUTIONS

Whether a room is too big or too small, oddly shaped or lacking definition, a sectional sofa can address almost any seating challenge. A large and substantial piece of furniture, it lends an immediate sense of permanence to an empty room, creates boundaries in an open loft, or offers ample seating in a cozy, conversational arrangement. Its modular design makes it easy to move—a big plus for apartment dwellers—making it easy to take advantage of every inch of a small space, where a traditional loveseat and sofa combination would waste valuable real estate.

The whole idea of a sectional sofa, and the reason for its devoted following, is flexibility. Sectional elements can be combined, like building blocks, to fit any living room's size or shape and any manner of mood or use. A slightly asymmetrical L is the most common shape—it both allows sitters to face each other in a more relaxed way and resolves potentially awkward corners of a room. U shapes and facing L's are also used to cradle a seating area and its sitters. A sectional's L can also grow with a family or be split up into two sofas.

Today, the sectional sofa has been adapted to almost every style of furniture and décor. At the high-style end of the spectrum, sofas such as B&B Italia's Harry and David Design's Hockney combine crisp, modern lines and innovative shapes with the sectional's flexibility. Shabby Chic offers white, slip-covered models, which can include extended and circular sections, while the Modulations Group makes a sofa comprising individual armchairs that can be detached for entertaining.

∧ INTIMATE
The comfortable scale and intimate arrangement of sectional sofas make them especially appealing to families

∧ JAUNTY ANGLES
The jaunty angles of the Nest sofa invite less rigid arrangements. By pulling this boxy couch away from the walls, the sofa's interesting back becomes a focal point of the room.

< ELEGANT PROPORTIONS
Paired with oversized art and simple accessories, the elegant proportions of Piero Lissoni's Nest sofa are perfectly balanced. Note how the cool metal hardware is warmed up by the lush, brown upholstery.

# A New Kind of Modern

**FRESH TAKE**

Combining a visible frame of chrome-plated or aluminum-gray lacquered steel with large, loose seat and back cushions, Piero Lissoni's Nest sofa offers a fresh take on midcentury modernism.

DIMENSIONS: AVAILABLE IN 72 IN. (183 CM) AND 126 IN. (320 CM) LENGTHS

---

## WHAT MAKES IT CLASSIC

- *A FRESH ANGLE: Informed by, but not limited to, midcentury modernism, the Nest sofa maximizes the simple lines and sheer size of minimalist furniture. The clean lines of the sofa are enhanced by the unexpected angles of its substantial cushions and the barely noticeable yet striking tubular-steel frame.*

- *VERSATILITY: Cassina makes the Nest sofa in three lengths, ranging from about 6 feet to 10 1/2 feet. Also available is an oversized chair version— Cassina calls it a love seat— as well as a matching bench and ottoman.*

The resurgence of modern and minimal styles in the late nineties paved the way for a new generation of sleek, functional furniture. One of the most beautiful pieces of lounge seating to come out of these recent years is Piero Lissoni's Nest sofa, designed for Cassina. Long, low-slung, and pure of line, the Nest can appear either formal or relaxed, depending on its surroundings.

The Nest is a contemporary interpretation of what the high-style modernism of the jet age was all about—or what it could have been. The sofa possesses some of the geometric rigor of modern fifties furniture, but it also sports unexpectedly jaunty angles, such as its flared back and jutting rear legs. With its deep, loose cushions, textured fabric, and, in the 10-foot version, sheer size, the Nest also shares the feeling of expansiveness and luxury found in sofas designed by Vladimir Kagan and Edward Wormley.

### A SOFA THAT HOLDS ITS OWN

Just as Kagan intended his large Serpentine sofa to simplify a room, the longest Nest (which seats six comfortably) can serve as the only piece of seating in a large space. The long, boxy body of the sofa rests lightly on a tubular steel frame—chrome-plated or painted aluminum gray—that is handsome enough to adorn the center of a living room. Underneath the sofa, the legs are set back more than 1 foot, making the already sleek piece appear to float above the floor.

Although no other seating may be necessary in a room filled with a 10-foot Nest, there are several pieces of furniture that complement it perfectly. A marble-topped, walnut credenza from Knoll, or one of the similar sideboards made by Cassina, will extend the clean lines and pure materials to the edge of a room. Add steel-legged coffee and side tables, such as Lissoni's Zap table, to match the sofa's contemporary look.

# An American Favorite

**OPULENT**
With its lush upholstery and signature hump, the distinctive camelback sofa adds sweeping curves and opulent comfort to even the most staid and mathematical of spaces.

DIMENSIONS: VARY

### WHAT MAKES IT CLASSIC

- *DIGNIFIED LOUNGING: Be it a rare antique, a faithful reproduction, or a completely new twist on the classic design, this is a couch that invites sitting and lounging without ever appearing sloppy.*

- *PERIOD DETAILS: Reproductions of period upholstery are available, for use both on the sofa and on throw pillows (though pillows are not an accurate period detail). Close reproductions of the original camelback are available, though modern versions, with deeper cushions and more familiar proportions, are often preferred.*

- *ENDURING APPEAL: Though the camelback was one of America's earliest sofas, it was eclipsed for most of the nineteenth century by more ornate European and Victorian styles. The sofa regained its stature, and popularity, at the turn of the twentieth century, when the first wave of the colonial revival inspired imitations of eighteenth-century homes and furnishings.*

The camelback sofa is perhaps the most venerable piece of lounge seating, and its air of aristocracy serves it well as the centerpiece of a traditional living room. Depending on the details and fabric, it can be the perfect Victorian settee or a bold addition to a modern, angular interior. Combining classical styling, absolute comfort, and timeless, graphic lines, it may just be the perfect couch.

Dating to the late eighteenth century, the camelback design speaks to the sensibilities of the Chippendale style and an era of fine American furniture. Some examples featured colonial claw and ball feet; almost all were characterized by gracefully scrolled arms and fine, elaborate upholstery.

### A COUCH THAT WORKS IN ALL CONTEXTS

In the centuries since, the camelback has become a fixture in American homes. The sofa's familiar form, central to American colonial style, has found its way into interiors ranging from country to postmodern. It works perfectly with similarly classic pieces of furniture: a pair of wing chairs, a tea table, or a highboy. But this classical form need not be limited to period interiors. The bold, graphic lines of the camelback sofa shine in modern, eclectic spaces. Modern interpretations—with thick, lush cushions, covered in new fabrics, bold colors, and even animal prints—have made it a unique feature in contemporary interior design.

∧ SIGNATURE CURVES
Named for the distinctive hump at its center,
the sofa extends the signature curves of
Chippendale chairs and tables to a longer,
upholstered form.

# classic tables

# Style and Substance

**CRAFTMANSHIP**

Simple, organic lines, noble woods, supreme craftsmanship, and substantial proportions define Frank Lloyd Wright's 1917 table. Designed for the Allen residence in Wichita, Kansas, the table's sturdy form and horizontal emphasis are indicative of Prairie School designs.

DIMENSIONS: H 28 IN. (70.5) CM X L 110 IN. (280 CM) X D 42 IN. (106 CM)

## WHAT MAKES IT CLASSIC

- *DIGNIFIED DEMEANOR: The Allen table's sturdy shape and solid demeanor make an impact. The rhythmic, vertical lines, combined with the strong, horizontal planes that typify the Prairie aesthetic, give the piece a quiet sense of importance.*

- *CRAFTSMANSHIP AND MATERIALS: A fine example of woodwork, the Allen table is constructed from solid hardwoods using traditional joiner's techniques. While Wright originally favored oak for its color and grain as well as its connotations of strength and durability, modern-day reproductions often are manufactured in natural or walnut-stained cherry.*

- *A PIECE OF HISTORY: Frank Lloyd Wright was a leader of the Prairie School, a group of Chicago architects who were closely tied to the American Arts and Crafts movement. In addition to designing some of the twentieth century's most famous buildings—the Larkin Building, Unity Temple, Fallingwater—Wright also developed everything from lighting to hardware to furnishings for his detailed interior schemes.*

The substantial profile and architectural lines of Frank Lloyd Wright's Allen table are more than just attractive. Historic yet modern, earthy yet linear, this massive, majestic piece easily and gracefully becomes the centerpiece of any room—perhaps the focal point of an entire home. A fine example of wood craftsmanship, this table can warm up a contemporary space.

## THE STRONG, SILENT TYPE

Designed in 1917, Frank Lloyd Wright's Allen table is based on the straight lines and rectilinear forms that its creator favored in the early part of his career. With a thick wooden top that extends beyond its simple upright supports, the Allen table relates to the low, ground-hugging, Prairie-style architecture that Wright pioneered in the Midwest. The table's blocky legs are equally substantial, making this piece both strong and stable. It is a classic design that reflects Wright's belief in simplicity and quality craftsmanship.

The Allen table is an excellent all-purpose piece that accommodates formal dining as well as daily meals. Its generous proportions make it comfortable, providing plenty of room for all. At home in an Arts and Crafts home as well as in more modern interiors, the Allen table works well in strong architectural spaces.

## DEFINING A SPACE

For loft dwellers, the Allen table's formidable presence helps define a dining area when there is no dining room per se. It is best paired with substantial chairs—of which Wright designed plenty—that are not likely to be overwhelmed by the table's heft. A high-back chair provides an elegant counterpoint to the table's pronounced horizontal lines.

Not surprisingly, this piece has made its way into libraries and offices, where its beautiful and ample work surface sees frequent use. Like other Wright tables, the Allen is also a popular and distinctive choice for reading rooms, conference rooms, and executive suites, where its sobriety and finely tuned craftsmanship convey a sense of dignity and prestige.

< LINEAR FORMS
Surrounded by a suite of Arts and Crafts chairs, Frank Lloyd Wright's Allen table grounds a long, open dining area. The table's blocky legs and substantial top, paired with the more linear forms of the chairs, creates a focal point for the room, lending the high-ceilinged space a solid foundation and a sense of intimacy.

# Easy Sophistication

**FAMILIAR AND FUTURISTIC**
With its basic round, laminated surface, and simple pedestal base, Eero Saarinen's 1956 table strikes a silhouette that is at once familiar and futuristic. The simple, cast aluminum base can be combined with a round or oval top in a choice of marble, wood, or laminate surfaces, to suit any room.

DIMENSIONS: W 41 IN. (104 CM) X H 28 IN. (70 CM)

**WHAT MAKES IT CLASSIC**

■ *TIMELESS SIMPLICITY: Although Saarinen's design is nearly fifty years old, this striking table seems as modern today as it did when it first appeared.*

■ *UNCLUTTERED AND PRACTICAL: As a dining table, Saarinen's table is unsurpassed in terms of practicality and efficiency—the simple, pedestal shape makes it easy to clean the floor underneath, while the spare, legless design offers ample room for lots of chairs.*

■ *AN INTEGRAL PART OF A ROOM: Saarinen once said that he created the Pedestal pieces not because he was interested in a particular shape, but because he was thinking about how furniture looked in a room. He intended for the Pedestal tables and chairs to work as a cohesive element in any room.*

The essence of simplicity in both form and function, the minimalist profile of Eero Saarinen's Pedestal table proves that calm, quiet lines and tough, no-nonsense materials can make an elegant design statement. Distilled to the point at which the essential parts—top and base—seem to meld into one, the Pedestal table is as efficient as it is attractive.

**MIDCENTURY MASTERPIECE**
Introduced in 1956, Eero Saarinen's Pedestal furniture reflects the Finnish-born architect's interest in unified, essential forms. A forward thinker, Saarinen was exhilarated by the newly available aluminum, plastic, and fiberglass and the possibilities they afforded. The tables in this innovative series feature round or oval tops of marble, wood, or laminate that are supported by cast aluminum bases. His signature flared base makes this group of tables modern, sculptural, and remarkably stable.

The simplicity of the form combined with the Saarinen's decision to use only the most essential materials result in a stunningly spare yet infinitely practical piece. The dining table is a particularly popular design that easily accommodates almost any variety of chair. The flared, metal base and thin-edged top give the table a sleek, futuristic look that adapts to both modern and traditional rooms.

**THE EPITOME OF VERSATILITY**
For those who favor midcentury modern, Saarinen's table is an obvious choice because it pairs well with matching tulip chairs or almost any of the other designs of that period, such as the Jacobsen, Eames, or Bertoia chairs. But the table's unique, sculptural shape and striking yet nondescript design make it a tasteful addition to more traditional interiors as well. Imagine its simple profile placed among overstuffed, living room furniture, or surrounded by garden-style, wrought iron chairs. When outfitted with a stately, marble top, it even works alongside formal antiques.

∧ CALM AND INVITING
A marble-topped Saarinen Pedestal table, surrounded with the designer's signature tulip
chairs, becomes the centerpiece of a modern
kitchen. While a more traditional set would have
generated a restless sea of legs—thirty-six legs
in all!—the pedestal design of both table and
chairs allows seating for eight, yet remains calm
and inviting. A smaller Saarinen side table in the
corner echoes the form of its larger sibling.

# Deco Deluxe

**MYRIAD USES**
Designed as a bedside table, Eileen Gray's adjustable table adjusts not only to a number of different heights, but myriad different uses. Comprising chrome-plated steel with a hardened glass top, it is the perfect bedside or chairside table, suitable to modern and contemporary interiors.

DIMENSIONS: W 22 IN. (56 CM) X H 24 IN. (62 CM) TO 39 IN. (100 CM) X D 15 IN. (39 CM)

---

**WHAT MAKES IT CLASSIC**

- *SIMPLE VERSATILITY: The E.1027 is the table that goes where tables aren't necessarily meant to go. Sturdy and stylish, it is the perfect pull-up table for breakfast in bed or tea on the sofa.*

- *A TOUCH OF COOL: The clean, modern lines of the E.1027 provide the perfect foil for warm, dark interiors. The gleam of chrome adds a bit of sparkle to lush upholstery, while the cantilever design makes it easy for the table to cozy right up to your favorite chair, sofa, or bed.*

- *THE DESIGNER'S TOUCH: Eileen Gray created the E.1027 table for the house that she designed for herself in the south of France. As with so many of her designs, the table folds, pivots, or adjusts to serve multiple functions and incorporates streamlined forms and machine-age materials.*

When you need a little table to serve multiple functions with style and ease, Eileen Gray's attractive and adaptable side table delivers. This sleek, deco design is made of tubular steel with an inset glass top that can be raised and lowered. It tucks under and cantilevers over a bed to hold a tray, making it an ideal bedside table. Carefully refined and ingeniously engineered, this inventive, modern classic combines beauty and versatility.

**BEYOND BEDSIDE**
A radically simple yet utterly original design, the E.1027 adapts to a range of contexts. As you might expect, this charming, functional table works well with other designs that also feature a strong sense of geometry, and it is very much at home with early modern pieces, such as Marcel Breuer's Wassily chair or Le Corbusier's Grand Confort sofa. Combining simplicity and precision, the E.1027 complements spare, contemporary interiors that require clean lines and slick materials. Yet it also works beautifully as an occasional table next to a sofa or club chair. With its lithe, cylindrical shape, the E.1027 lends a sense of balance and refinement to today's large-scale, squared-off furnishings.

< LINEAR FORM
Beside a comfortable club chair, Gray's gleaming E.1027 creates a gentle contrast with warm upholstery. The tables minimal, linear form makes it a functional side table without taking up a lot of space—a great feature in a smaller room.

# Tray Chic

Perhaps best associated with TV dinners of the fifties, the classic tray table—a portable snack table that featured removable trays on folding wooden stands—becomes a perfect accent piece when approached with a designer's eye for detail and attention to form. Juxtaposing warm, rich leather with polished nickel, Thomas O'Brien's Wooster tray table is a chic, modern take on this once ubiquitous form. These stunning little tables, once tossed in closets until called into action for a meal in front of the television, earn a permanent place in any room as accent tables, side tables, even cocktail tables.

### WARM SURFACES

The familiar form of the tray table goes from mundane practicality to high style when executed in buttery leather and polished nickel. The sturdier base and warm surface make the Wooster tray table an attractive table for everyday use.

DIMENSIONS: W 14 IN. (36 CM) X D 13.5 IN. (34 CM) X H 20 IN. (51 CM) IS AVERAGE

### SMALL WONDER

O'Brien's brand of "warm modernism" brings together midcentury forms and classic pieces to create a comfortable, inviting atmosphere. A versatile option for many different room settings, the Wooster tray table is an elegant little accent or side table that can also serve as stylish bedside table. Where space is limited, a pair of these sleek, smart tables can even stand in for a coffee table. The table's tooled-leather tray top has a stitched cross detail that resonates with the X-shaped base. Cool and sophisticated, this piece bridges the traditional and the modern with its luxurious materials and linear silhouette.

### WHAT MAKES IT CLASSIC

- *ADAPTABLE AND PORTABLE: Easily moved to serve different functions, the tray table is the rare piece that combines utility with high style.*

- *DESIGNED FOR LIVING: While the original tray tables were lightweight and collapsible for storage, O'Brien's updated version is a more stable design that is better suited for everyday use.*

- *SIGNATURE STYLE: New York–based designer Thomas O'Brien is known for his skilled juxtaposition of eclectic furniture and objects. Guided not by the dictates of fashion but by a disciplined eye, O'Brien appreciates sensuous materials and elegant details as much as he admires down-to-earth simplicity and pragmatic utility.*

The Wooster tray table adds a sensuous, modern edge to traditional interiors and a hint of understated luxury to pared-down, contemporary rooms. Its small scale and delicate look work exceptionally well it small spaces. Paired with a substantial club chair, the tray table completes a simple reading nook, providing a perfect surface for a reading lamp, small stack of books, and a cup of tea or snifter of cognac.

∧ COUNTERPOINT
In a grand space grounded by modern upholstered furnishings, the lightweight, linear form
of the Wooster tray table provides a striking
counterpoint. The rich leather surface and
bright nickel legs complement the inviting and
luxurious feel of the room while creating a
simple, dignified contrast with the sofa and
chairs' heavier silhouettes.

# The Luxury of Simplicity

**MOBILE**

With its wood plank top, finished with age-old methods, and its thoroughly modern, totally mobile wheeled steel legs, the D'Urso supper table is a rare combination of minimalist practicality and traditional substance.

DIMENSIONS: L 96 IN. (244 CM) x W 32 IN. (81 CM) x H 28 IN. (71 CM)

**WHAT MAKES IT CLASSIC**

- *MODERNISM THAT IMPROVES WITH AGE: The table's kiln-dried wooden top is finished with tung oil and wax, enabling the surface to age beautifully and naturally.*

- *A MULTIFUNCTION TABLE: An excellent option for home-office environments, the supper table can do double duty as a desk and a dining table.*

- *INFLUENTIAL DESIGNER: Joe D'Urso is among a handful of designers who popularized minimalism during the seventies. D'Urso's early furniture and interiors has influenced the renewed interest in minimalist design*

< PERFECT SOLUTIONS

Defined by its relatively lightweight design and practical casters, the D'Urso supper table is the perfect solution for a studio apartment or double-duty home office/dining area. Attractive, with relatively small proportions, it can seat eight people for a dinner party one night, then wheel back up against a wall to function as a desk the next morning.

The basic elements of the table are boiled down to their very essence, then improved upon, in this utterly simple yet functional and inviting table. Warm wood planks meet practical metal legs and casters, and the table becomes a moveable work of art, suitable for home or office, and just about anywhere in between.

An early champion of minimalism, designer Joe D'Urso is still known for his rigorously contemporary aesthetic. As his supper table illustrates, minimalism is, for D'Urso, not merely a style, but a studied method of extracting the beauty and essence of any given piece. In this case, three solid-milled wooden planks comprise the table's top, which is supported by a blackened steel base with wheels. With its classic simplicity, D'Urso's supper table has a distinctly modern look.

**HIGH ROLLER**

Mounted on rubber-wheel casters, the supper table provides a mobile dining or work surface that is generously scaled and thoughtfully detailed. Perfect for a loft, apartment, or any space that demands flexibility, this table design can be easily moved to serve multiple purposes. D'Urso's collage-like use of materials—thick, oiled and waxed mahogany or oak combined with blackened steel or brushed stainless steel—reflects an expert balance of warm, natural, and cold industrial elements.

The supper table's straightforward, functional design and complementary materials make this a versatile piece that can work with numerous seating options. Equally simple chairs, such as the Emeco chair or Mario Bellini's Cab chair, play off of the table's informal, urban style. The table can be wheeled over to a sofa to create a temporary banquette or repositioned to serve as a work table with minimum effort.

# The New Classicism

Combining traditional forms with modern sensibilities, Michael Vanderbyl's Archetype dining table speaks to a variety of influences, from the classical themes of ancient Greece and Rome to the striking modernism of the thirties. An oval dining table with four tapered legs, each fitted with a metal caster, this elegant piece gives new form to traditional motifs and shapes, making it suitable for almost any interior, from an ultramodern loft to a neoclassical parlor.

## BEAUTY AND BALANCE

Notable for its strong architectural lines and extreme restraint, Vanderbyl's entire archetype collection emphasizes sophisticated design for formal and modern interiors. Veneered with richly figured English sycamore and available in a deep-toned or light finish, his dining table is highly adaptable to numerous schemes.

With its precise detailing and balanced proportions, the dining table can blend seamlessly into a room dominated with fine antiques. At the same time, the table's classical geometry and straight lines—emphasized by its elegant tapered legs—can work with a more contemporary aesthetic. Free of complex decoration and superfluous ornament, this table works with Deco-influenced decor as well as transitional modern designs. The embodiment of balance and repose, it is suited to a formal arrangement of flowers set in an antique urn; yet a more spare arrangement of calla lilies or even just a scattering of small votive candles take the table in an entirely different direction.

### INVESTMENT

Elegant lines and timeless design make Michael Vanderbyl's Archetype dining table an investment for the ages. Suitable to a number of formal interiors, its clean lines and simple profile appeal to give it a modern yet classical form.

DIMENSIONS: H 30 IN. (76 CM) x D 42 IN. (107 CM) x L 82 IN. (208 CM)

### WHAT MAKES IT CLASSIC

- *IN ELEGANT COMPANY: Paired with Vanderbyl's elegant Archetype chairs, it creates a timeless dining suite. Juxtaposed with a collection of mismatched but interesting chairs finished in distressed paint, and the table transforms itself into the essence of eclectic chic.*

- *OPTIONAL FINISHES: While the table's dark finish option resonates with French and English pieces, the pale-toned alternative approaches a Biedermeier look. Either version complements schemes that incorporate simple geometry and clean lines.*

- *NOBLE ROOTS: Neoclassicism is most often associated with the French Empire style popularized by Napoleon in the early 1800s. A style that incorporates the classical motifs of ancient Greece and Rome, the Empire style was designed to give credibility and legitimacy to Napoleon's regime.*

∧ CENTER STAGE
Anchored by the dignified form of Michael
Vanderbyl's classic dining table, this formal dining room incorporates other elements from the
designer's Archetype collection. The pale walls
and simple window treatments allow the rich
wood of the chairs, credenza, and table to take
center stage.

The sculptural form of the Noguchi table creates
an effective juxtaposition with harder-edged surroundings. Paired with clean, linear furnishings,
the table's clear glass surface highlights the stunning walnut base and provides an attractive surface on which to display additional works of art.

# Artistic Edge

**ART AT WORK**
Combining an Eastern-influenced modern design with organic forms, Isamu Noguchi's classic coffee table is the essence of art at work. The elemental lines and attention to materials that characterize the Noguchi coffee table speak to the designer's Japanese-American experience and love of natural forms.

DIMENSIONS: H 8 IN. (20 CM) X D 36 IN. (91.4 CM) X L 50 IN. (127 CM)

## WHAT MAKES IT CLASSIC

- *FUNCTIONAL ART: With its stunning sculptural form and contrasting elements of glass and walnut, the Noguchi table could serve as a work of art all by itself. Yet its simple shape and materials work well as a display surface for a variety of objets d'art.*

- *A MARRIAGE OF INFLUENCES: Isamu Noguchi's upbringing in Japan and the United States informed the unique vision that he brought to his designs for gardens, interiors, and lighting. His dedication to natural materials, skilled craftsmanship, and biomorphic forms is evident in all of his work. With its simple, sculptural shape, the coffee table, in particular, demonstrates Noguchi's distinctive marriage of these interests and influences.*

- *A LONG HISTORY: Herman Miller introduced Noguchi's coffee table in 1947 and produced it in a variety of woods until 1973. Due to popular demand, this piece was reissued in 1984 and is still in production today.*

Natural materials breathe life into Isamu Noguchi's 1947 minimalist, biomorphic coffee table. The sculptural tripod base, comprising two interlocking pieces of solid walnut, provides the focal point and is highlighted by the rounded, triangular slab of clear, 3/4-inch glass that forms the table's top. Artful, yet utterly simple, the unit is a striking presence in any setting.

## EASTERN SIMPLICITY MEETS WESTERN MODERISM

The simplicity of this classic, modern table makes it an extremely versatile piece. It adds a cool, modern twist to Asian-inspired interiors and provides an interesting foil for Eastern antiques. While this piece is at home with other modern designs, it provides a warmth and softness that some twentieth-century furniture lacks. The table's distinctive shape and simplified elements work equally well with tubular steel chairs, such as Marcel Beuer's Cesca chair, and alongside traditional Asian pieces.

Today the table's walnut base is available with a natural or ebony stain, which changes the look of the table significantly. The natural walnut complements other wooden pieces—old or new—while the ebony stain offers more drama and contrast to a room. Either way, the coffee table's curvaceous, asymmetrical shape is a welcome relief from the squared and rigorously symmetrical furniture so popular now. For this reason, Noguchi's classic design remains a fresh and inspired original.

# Farm Fresh

**CLASSIC**
Its honest, functional design and sturdy materials make the farm table a classic in almost any interior.

DIMENSIONS: W 36 IN. (91 CM) x L 84 IN. (213 CM) IS AVERAGE

## WHAT MAKES IT CLASSIC

- *LONGEVITY: This design has been around for more than three centuries, and with good reason. Beautiful and adaptable, this table performs as well for you as it did for your great-great-grandmother.*

- *TOUGH MATERIALS: Farm tables are typically made of pale-toned, close-grained fruit woods, such as cherry or pear. These woods are inexpensive and fairly hard, but they also are easily worked and well-suited for furniture. As an additional bonus, they acquire a rich, stunning patina with heavy use.*

- *OLD WORLD UTILITY: Offering little in the way of ornament, farm tables often feature useful additions such as a pull-out groaning board.*

The farm table is a humble, hard-working piece that epitomizes Old World charm. The sturdy, rectangular table that has become a much-coveted classic most likely dates back to the late eighteenth or early nineteenth century. Typically made of light-toned fruit woods, this rustic, substantial table generally is unadorned, but it almost always features artfully turned legs that lend it character.

## RUSTIC CHARM

A perennial favorite for country-style interiors, the farm table is making its way into contemporary schemes, too, where its organic materials and solid form add substance to slicker, more modern accessories. When matched with contrasting textures—such as metal chairs or fine bone china—this Old World charmer becomes the centerpiece of an eclectic setting. Consider surrounding this farm-inspired masterpiece with more edgy chairs, such as the aluminum Emeco chair.

## DINING ROOM AND BEYOND

Whether a genuine antique or a quality reproduction, the sturdy French farm table offers exceptional craftsmanship and a surface and finish that tend to improve with wear. Its rugged good looks and timeless profile make this table a perfect choice for casual meals in an informal dining room or eat-in kitchen. Virtually indestructible and incredibly stable, it works equally well as a dining table for families as well as a prep area in a kitchen with limited counter space. Surrounded by chairs or lined with long, rustic benches, it is the ultimate table for informal, group dining. Move it into the home office, and it's the perfect writing table or desk, adding warmth to a space often dominated by modern machinery and cold textures.

∧ SLEEK INTERPRETATION
With its simple legs and oblong shape, this elegant dining table offers a sleek interpretation of the classic French farm table. The polished, hardworking form blends well with a variety of different styles, from classic French country interiors to eclectic interiors.

< AIRY SIMPLICITY
The table's design highlights the graceful angles of its bent birch frame, creating a vision of airy simplicity that is never cold or austere.

# Scandinavian Simplicity

**ELEGANT LEGS**
Simple yet stunning, the bent beechwood legs of the Aalto L-Leg table make it geometric, yet fluid. The elegantly shaped legs echo the forms of Aalto's popular stools and chairs.

DIMENSIONS: VARY

### WHAT MAKES IT CLASSIC

- *CLEAN MATERIALS: The simple form of the L-Leg table is enhanced by Aalto's use of clear glass and bright, tidy birch wood. Easily worked and enhanced by polishing, birch is especially suitable for slender profiles and takes on a deep, golden yellow tone.*

- *A DIVERSE COLLECTION: Aalto's L-Leg collection, which includes chairs, stools, and tables, was developed in the early thirties and has been a popular favorite ever since.*

- *ORIGINS: Architect Alvar Aalto is said to have derived his interest in wooden furniture from the ubiquitous birch forests of his native Finland. His early experimentation with molded birch plywood resulted in numerous furniture designs notable for their practical simplicity.*

Lightweight yet strong and durable, Alvar Aalto's exquisite L-Leg table offers a pared-down simplicity that is a hallmark of twentieth-century Scandinavian design. Between 1933 and 1935, Aalto developed a series of these tables in different sizes for the Viipuri Library that was distinguished by solid birch legs with a laminated 90-degree bend. As with much of Aalto's work, the tables in this group have slender, modern silhouettes and inherent warmth.

### A SIMPLE SOLUTION
The cool, friendly materials and economy of design exemplified by Aalto's L-Leg table make it an adaptable addition to a number of different interior schemes. The dining tables in this group are strikingly simple and perfect for casual settings where practicality and function are important. They make great family dining tables, as they can withstand everyday use. At the same time, the L-Leg table offers an elegant, understated simplicity that can lend it to more formal environments.

Aalto designed numerous seating options to go with his table for those who are interested in a pure Scandinavian aesthetic. L-Leg stools accentuate the tables' humble simplicity, while his webbed chairs provide an interesting, textural counterpoint. The Jacobsen chair's undulating curves and lively range of colors also work well with the L-Leg table's clean lines and pale, wood tone.

# Pure Grace

## SIMPLICITY

With its clean, simple lines and pure attention to function, this stunning dining table by Thomas Moser is the essence of Shaker simplicity. With the addition of two leaves, the table extends from a mere 72 inches (183 CM) to a generous 116 inches (295 CM), with room for ten comfortable diners.

DIMENSIONS: OVAL TABLE SHOWN IS L 72 IN. (183 CM) X H 30 IN. (76 CM) X W 48 IN. (122 CM)

## WHAT MAKES IT CLASSIC

- *ACCESSIBILITY: A number of contemporary furniture makers have revived the Shaker tradition and are offering faithful reproductions and reinterpretations of the classic design.*

- *ADAPTABILITY: While puritan values inform the foundations of Shaker design, the integrity of the Shaker form is as modern as the most exuberant twenty-first-century furnishings.*

- *AN AMERICAN CLASSIC: The Shakers were nineteenth-century America's largest and best-known communal society. The simple designs that their religious beliefs inspired are enduring for their beauty and fine craftsmanship.*

Rooted in Puritan austerity and honed by exceptional craftsmanship and artistic vision, the Shaker aesthetic embodies a radical sparseness that approaches minimalism. The tables that the Shakers crafted for dining and work purposes exemplify their devotion to pious simplicity and honest work. Made of humble woods, such as pine and maple, these pieces are wholly utilitarian, yet extremely graceful.

## SIMPLE BUT NOT SIMPLISTIC

The simplicity of the Shaker tables makes them extremely versatile. Noticeably fine and elegantly proportioned, these noble pieces whisper quality. The humble nature of the tables makes them ideal for family dining, but they can also serve as generous worktables.

Shaker tables naturally complement early American antiques, but their delicate proportions and clean lines make them suitable for a variety of surroundings with equal grace. Their design conveys a contemporary sensibility that is well-suited to spare, modern interiors, while their unpretentious presence can add a fresh counterpoint in densely decorated spaces.

In a dining area, these tables are best paired with high-backed, Shaker-style chairs to create a coherent ensemble. But for those who appreciate the Shaker style more than the Shaker sobriety, the chairs' webbed seats and backs can be enlivened with fun, bright colors. Use a different color for each chair to create a whimsical, kaleidoscopic effect that offsets the table's rigorously pragmatic design.

∧ MODEST FORM

The timeless proportions and simple design of
this stunning Shaker table make it the perfect
dining table in just about any interior. Its modest form does not compete with the surroundings, allowing the antique rug and rustic texture
of the stone fireplace to shine. The rich wood
provides a perfect surface for the formal candle-
sticks—to cover this table with linens would be
a crime.

Sleigh Bed

Trundle Bed

Futon Bed

Waterbed

Murphy Bed

Daybed

Canopy Bed

Four-Post Bed

Bunk Bed

Iron Bed

classic beds

# The Bed for Any Bedroom

**CENTERPIECE**
The gentle curves and weighty proportions of the sleigh bed make it the perfect centerpiece for almost any bedroom.

DIMENSIONS: W 59 IN. (150 CM) X L 97 IN. (246 CM) IS AVERAGE

## WHAT MAKES IT CLASSIC

- *A TURN OF THE SHEET: With just a change of bed linens, this bed is reborn. Laid with spartan white sheets and comforter, it lends a room a summery feel. A country quilt provides a dainty sense of charm, while an ensemble of dark gentleman's plaids allow this piece to make itself at home in a rustic atmosphere.*

- *TRANSPORTATION INSPIRATION: The sleigh bed got its name from its resemblance to the horse-drawn sleds of the nineteenth century. Created as part of the American Empire–style of furniture, it borrows its shape from the French lit en bateau: a bed whose headboard and footboard are shaped like the prow of a boat. In fact, the sleigh bed was once also often referred to as a gondola or boat bed.*

- *SECRETS OF THE ANTIQUE SLEIGH BED: Period sleigh beds—designed to sit lengthwise against a wall—are often decorated only on one side. Modern versions boast overall ornamentation.*

Victorian travelers got around in snowy weather by tucking themselves into a horsedrawn sleigh and covering up with cozy blankets. Inspired by this romantic notion of comfort, the sleigh bed—with its high, scrolled headboard and footboard joined by deep, integral side rails—takes the sleigh concept out of the snow and into the home. Ever versatile, this bed works well in any context, be it an English country cottage or a contemporary townhouse filled with a mix of modern and antique furnishings.

The sleigh bed is the one bed that suits any style. It possesses graceful curves and yet a weighty feel and architectural presence, making it a design that is neither masculine nor feminine, old nor new. And with a number of interpretations available—from deep mahogany interpretations with ornate scrollwork, to simple, Shaker-inspired slatted versions, to space-conscious iterations constructed from wrought iron—there is indeed a sleigh to suit any décor.

## A DEFINING PRESENCE

Take your cue on where to place a sleigh bed from the shape and construction of the bed. The design was devised to be perched lengthwise along a wall, daybed style; the addition of a multitude of large, lush pillows transforms the twin-sized bed into an attractive settee. But this stunning sleeper is no wallflower. The large proportions and sculptural form give the bed—especially queen of king-sized examples—a potent sense of presence. So it works equally well in the middle of a large space, where it easily becomes the centerpiece of a loft or studio. You can create a sense of privacy and revive an age-old tradition by enclosing the bed in draperies from above, perhaps updating the look with a simple, homemade canopy of mosquito netting or sheer organza.

∧ SLEEK
Barbara Barry's updated interpretation of the
sleigh bed emphasizes the style's traditional
curves while offering a sleeker, more architectural
profile. The bed's deep color and bold angles
provide an interesting counterpoint to the room's
traditional moldings and draperies without ever
appearing modern or minimalist.

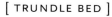

# The Single Bed Built for Two

In smaller homes short on bedrooms, or in houses where the guest room has been sacrificed to make room for home offices, finding additional sleeping space can be a challenge. Enter the trundle bed, a charming bit of centuries-old ingenuity that offers sleeping space for two in the space of a single twin bed. Tucked beneath a daybed, or even a bare-bones bed frame, a trundle offers all the comfort of a regular mattress without taking up precious floor space.

## A KID'S-ROOM SOLUTION

In a room shared by two children or, perhaps, occupied by just one child who enjoys sleepovers, the trundle is a solution to sleep-space shortages. Tucking one bed beneath the other leaves lots of play space on the floor that would have been eaten up by a second bed. When opened, the beds can sit snugly together, step style, creating a safety zone for children prone to falling out of bed. Alternatively, the bed can be easily rolled across the room if siblings do not wish to sleep quite so close together.

## A SECRET GUEST BED

In a guest room, too, the trundle is a hardworking piece of furniture, offering room for two guests in the space of a single twin bed. Whether it's grandma or your son's best friend who's spending the night, the trundle bed offers a comfortable place to sleep without your having to permanently give up valuable real estate or exile guests to the sofa.

The trundle's two-for-one practicality is especially useful in guest rooms that serve double duty as a sewing room or home office. These compact designs can be dressed up as sofas until overnight visitors call them into action.

Today, manufacturers offer trundle features to suit any décor and sense of style. Although it is often designed for kids' spaces with whimsical motifs, the trundle also comes in more mature designs—including sleigh beds, daybeds, iron beds, and other styles.

## CELESTIAL MOTIF

The perfect kids'-room solution, the trundle provides an extra bed without eating up valuable floor space. This charming wooden version—decorated with a celestial motif—is sturdy enough to withstand lots of active play.

DIMENSIONS: W 44 IN. (112 CM) X L 77 IN. (196 CM) X H 24 IN. (61 CM) IS AVERAGE

## WHAT MAKES IT CLASSIC

- *PRAGMATIC AND COMFORTABLE: Simple practicality and charming dimensions combine to make the trundle bed in any of its forms the perfect solution for the space deprived.*

- *CLASSICAL INSPIRATIONS: The trundle bed was developed in the fifteenth century for live-in servants. In royal households, the trundle bed went to a servant of rank. In the queen's room, for example, the first maid of honor would occupy it.*

- *CROSS-CULTURAL HISTORY: Though the trundle bed was originally a gothic design, it is more popularly associated with early American and colonial homes, where, like its function today, it helped solve issues of limited space.*

< LESS SPACE
While the trundle can be tucked away when not in use, these two young sisters have chosen to dress it up in pretty linens and quilts and leave it open, giving each child her own bed, yet using less space than two separate twin beds.

# East Meets West

**ZENLIKE AESTHETIC**
With its soft cushion and firm base, the futon-and-platform combination provides the healthful benefits and Zenlike aesthetic of the traditional futon, while appealing to Western sensibilities by raising the bed off the floor.

DIMENSIONS: VARY

### WHAT MAKES IT CLASSIC

- *A BETTER BED: The futon is the bed, boiled down to the only thing it really needs to be: a comfortable place to sleep. The softness of the futon, produced by layers of cotton batting, gets a dose of firm support from the floor beneath, making it a healthful place to rest.*

- *A BETTER SOFA BED: Infinitely more comfortable than a standard sofa bed, the futon/frame combination offers a nice solution to studio dwellers who need a bed that can double as a couch.*

- *AN ADAPTABLE STYLE: Recognizing the popularity of the futon/frame combination, furniture producers now offer frames in a number of styles, from Stickley-inspired Mission examples to sleigh beds.*

Spare and functional, the futon is an essential design in Asian-infused interiors, bringing a Zenlike sense of calm to the bedroom. But long before twentieth-century modernists "invented" minimalism, Japanese homes were the definition of simplicity in form and function. With space always at a premium, the Japanese eschewed the use of large and cumbersome beds and instead slept on futons. Arranged directly on the floor (over a carpet of tatami mats) for sleeping, these mats of quilted padding with a cotton coverlet could easily be rolled up and stored during the day. Their flexibility in form and function makes them equally appealing for today's homeowners, no matter where they live.

### VARIATIONS THAT MAKE SENSE

Although this traditional bed has been used for centuries in Japan, it has been tailored for Western sensibilities since it was introduced in the States in the 1940s. Futons sold in the United States are usually thicker, and are perched on some sort of frame or platform, rather than laid out on the floor. Some platforms raise the bed only a few inches and may be larger than the futon itself (often with a base of tatami) in order to maintain the traditional Japanese look while appealing to westerners' ideas about where one should sleep.

The futon's range of uses in the West is another departure from its original Asian inspiration. Wood or metal frames support futons, allowing them to serve double duty as sofas or loveseats. Futons that fold in this manner must utilize a core of some kind (usually made of foam or wool) to provide the support that keeps them from collapsing.

∧ NATURAL ADDITION
With its low profile and minimalist appeal, the
futon-and-platform combination is a natural
addition to a spare, modern bedroom like this
one. Devoid of any ornamentation, the bed
leaves the room's architecture to speak for itself,
and allows the other furnishings—from plants
to artwork—to take center stage.

∧ ELEGANT WATERBED
With its minimalist design and simple, ground-hugging design, this elegant waterbed has combines the spare aesthetic of a futon and platform with the comfort and health benefits that only a waterbed can provide. Paired with a sophisticated wrought-iron screen, it creates a peaceful but welcoming atmosphere.

# Aquatic Style

**EXPANDING THE RANGE**
Although classic waterbeds have a distinctly Asian look, designers are now also producing waterbeds that replicate the look of more traditional beds, expanding the range of decorating options.

DIMENSIONS: VARY

## WHAT MAKES IT CLASSIC

- *STYLE AND SUBSTANCE: The body is 90 percent water, and many New Age theorists site returning to water as a way to induce inner calm. Waterbeds embrace that idea with practical comfort and intriguing designs.*

- *ANCIENT PRECEDENTS: The first waterbeds were actually used by the Persians more than 3,600 years ago in the form of goatskins filled with water. Even the Romans had a primitive version of the waterbed; for them it consisted of lying in a cradle of warm water until feeling sleepy and then being lifted onto a rocking mattress.*

- *A HEALTHY HISTORY: The waterbed as we know it today was a nineteenth-century invention, created for use in hospitals for patients who suffered from bed sores, bone fractures, or paralysis. The modern waterbed used in the home was first patented in 1853 in England. It resembled a mattress-sized hot-water bottle and was sold through Harrods' mail-order catalog.*

In the sixties and seventies, the waterbed was the centerpiece of the groovy bachelor pad, the ultimate accessory for swinging singles. But the waterbed's appeal is more practical and pedestrian than the hype indicates. The soothing, womblike quality of the water-filled mattress cradles the sleeper in comfort.

The waterbed's popularity may have waned since its free-love heyday, but the medicinal benefits that a waterbed provides—including even, unsagging support for the spine and improved circulation—make it a favorite of many people. Modern improvements like leak-proof liners, heaters, and interior baffles that control the motion of the water have made this style of bed once again fashionable.

**AN UNTRADITIONAL PIECE THAT'S ENTIRELY ADAPTABLE**
Produced from large, flexible plastic cushions filled with water, waterbeds are most commonly contained in a low, boxlike wooden frame. The design works well with spare interiors dominated by broad horizontal planes. Indeed, the bed had a low profile—because it is tucked neatly inside its modified platform frame—that offers a soothing, Zenlike quality. Add a built-in headboard in your choice of cabinetry styles for a custom look.

**GRANDIOSE**

At bedtime, the Murphy bed has all the character of a grandiose headboard; during the day, it tucks away into a cabinet that makes an attractive statement on its own.

DIMENSIONS: VARY

### WHAT MAKES IT CLASSIC

- *A PRIVATE HIDEAWAY: The Murphy bed not only clears the floor for dancing, it provides some degree of separation between the sleep area and the rest of the apartment, a meaningful feature for studio dwellers who dream of a private bedroom.*

- *A CENTURY OF SECRET BEDS: Murphy filed the first patent for his design in 1900 and perfected it eight years later. The popularity of Murphy beds has fluctuated with the home buyer's market, but the bed's charm has always made it a selling point for those working with small spaces.*

- *EARLY PRECEDENTS. Though the Murphy bed is a twentieth-century invention, folding beds with legs that came out from furniture or architectural elements are said to have originated in the eighteenth century, with models that disappeared behind a bookcase, chest, or liquor cabinet.*

# The Secret Hideaway

There is something magic about a Murphy bed. While most beds are simply there, the Murphy bed seems not to be there, until it unveils itself: Doors swing open, and down falls a big, comfy mattress out of what looked like a regular old closet. The Murphy bed seems to know that the bed concealed is perhaps more intriguing than the bed that is available for all to see. A glimpse of a Murphy bed being pulled out or tucked away always draws smiles.

### WHEN SPACE IS AN ISSUE

Today's apartment dwellers often opt for a Murphy bed for the same reason William L. Murphy invented it in the early part of the twentieth century. Wishing to entertain in his one-room apartment, Murphy began experimenting with a foldaway bed so that he'd have more room for parties. In a tiny space, the Murphy bed is still the best answer to that same plight. It offers a full-size mattress, is more comfortable than a pull-out sofa bed, and tucks tidily away in a wall-hugging closet.

The bed is usually tucked behind paneled closet doors, though units that look like bookcases are becoming popular, as well. The closet itself can be built-in or freestanding (although always bolted to the wall), and may be designed to complement the décor of the room, with crown moldings and fine trim.

∧ DISCREET
The genius of the Murphy bed is it ability to go completely unnoticed. With its Murphy bed tucked discreetly away, this small space becomes a wide open gallery.

< ANYTHING BUT TEMPORARY
Pulled out from a built-in closet, this Murphy bed looks anything but temporary. By painting the interior of the closet with deep blue paint, outfitting the bed with matching blue linens and a fabric-covered headboard, and outfitting the space complementary end tables, this homeowner has created additional room that disappears when the bed is tucked away.

∧ CHARMING ADDITION
With its simple profile and stunning tufted cushions, this elegant daybed takes its styling cues from the earliest examples of the form. Interesting and unexpected, it makes a charming addition to a formal room, providing a surprising invitation to put one's feet up and relax.

# Beds That Don't Need Bedrooms

**UNIQUE CHARM**
Simple lines and charming beadboard panels give this simple daybed unique charm. Even devoid of pillows, it seems more sofa than bed; yet its soothing profile invites serious lounging.

DIMENSIONS: VARIES; CAN BE H 39 IN. (99 CM) x D 42 IN. (107 CM) x L 81 IN. (206 CM)

## WHAT MAKES IT CLASSIC

- *A FAMILY FAVORITE: Daybeds are popular in modern homes, offering both a place to sleep and to sit. When combined with a trundle, they are particularly well suited to children's rooms, as well as home offices, dens, and other spaces that double as guest rooms.*

- *A PLACE TO REST: The daybed was first introduced as seating in the seventeenth century. Originally called a* Lit de repos, *French for "rest bed," the daybed was intended as a place where a person could comfortably recline for quiet contemplation.*

- *AN EVOLVING FORM: The long, elegant shape of the daybed has taken many forms. Today, the term* daybed *usually refers not to a chaise lounge or sofa but to an actual bed with a same-height foot and headboard, and often a backboard.*

If a bed is a place to sleep for the night, then where is one to nap during the day? Enter the daybed, which invites reclining and daydreaming, curling up with a book, or indulging in a midday snooze. In a bedroom, den, or living area, this is a stylish but hardworking piece of furniture. Useful as an extra bed, it also shines as a sofa. Add one to a master bedroom to give the kids a place to curl up for story time or movie watching or to sleep on scary, stormy nights. In a studio apartment, daybeds offer space-saving solutions for seating and sleeping. Children love them as beds and also enjoy having their own little sofa during the day. In a den, drawing room, or media room, daybeds provide the perfect place to kick back and relax.

Available in interpretations ranging from neoclassical to high Victorian to stately Arts and Crafts iterations, there is truly a daybed for any space and any purpose.

### CLASSICAL FOUNDATIONS, DESIGNER INSPIRATIONS
The daybed concept is most likely borrowed from the bed that was developed in classical Greece and Rome as a place to recline during mealtimes. But the daybed as we know it, in its earliest design, has a headrest that became a sloping chair back. It was heavily adorned with ornamentation and had hinged arms that converted into a headrest at each end, with an extended, upholstered seat often supported by as many as eight legs.

While the daybed is related to the chaise lounge and couch—and is often confused with both—it is its own style of furniture. It has become a favorite design in modern furniture collections, most notably designer Eileen Gray's minimalist interpretation and the Barcelona daybed. Often used as seating for living rooms or for drama in a boudoir, the daybed continues to symbolize luxury and relaxation.

# Adding a Touch of Romance

Sweeping curves, layers of rich or sheer fabric, the natural beauty of hand-turned wood—few pieces of furniture speak to romance quite like a canopy bed. Designed for privacy, these stunning beds allude to the intimate nature of the bedroom, and infuse grand bedrooms with a regal air.

A canopy bed has a fabric roof most commonly supported by four posts. The canopy can also consist of fabric that is suspended from a wall, a set of corner posts, or, as originally designed, the ceiling (a variation called a *sparver*). Today, a canopy bed is usually a four-poster bed, with a frame joining the posts at the top, from which a fabric valance is hung. Available in modern interpretations as well as eighteenth-century reproductions, the large scale and undeniable presence of canopy beds make a large impact in any bedroom or suite.

## STUNNING

With hand-turned and hand-carved posts, this stunning canopy bed is a faithful reproduction of an eighteenth-century British design attributed to Thomas Sheraton and George Hepplewhite.

DIMENSIONS VARY: SHERATON FIELD BED WITH REEDED POSTS (SHOWN) HAS POSTS THAT ARE 67 IN. (169 CM) HIGH AND A 20 IN. (51 CM) RAIL

## WHAT MAKES IT CLASSIC

- *CHARMING VARIATIONS: By changing the fabric draperies—from a simple crocheted coverlet, for example, to a billowing cloud of sheer organza—the canopy can be easily transformed to suit the room, the occupant, or the season.*

- *PRACTICAL CONSIDERATIONS: The canopy was originally conceived in the eleventh-century as a means of creating seclusion—not to mention protection from dust and insects. In fact, the word* canopy *derived from the Greek term for "a net to keep the out gnats."*

- *ROYAL ROOTS: In its early days, the canopy was a symbol of status. Only high-ranking household members had beds with a full canopy. Others' canopies would only partially cover the bed (in a variation called Angel beds).*

## SOFTENING A FORMAL LOOK

But the canopy idea is not limited to grand master bedrooms decorated with antiques for Old World charm. Many homeowners opt to create more informal valances by draping fabric over dowels hung from the ceiling, or gathering a curtain of fabric around an embroidery hoop suspended above the head of the bed. Such options allow homeowners to replicate the regal and romantic feel of the canopy bed in a more updated fashion.

Canopies also lend themselves to children's rooms. Attached to a baby's crib or cradle, they make a beautiful statement in the nursery. In a little girl's bedroom, they speak of princesses and fairy tales.

∧ RESTRAINED OPULENCE
This elegant bed contrasts stunning, turned
posts and an ornate headboard with a low, simple footboard and spare canopy. The effect is
one of restrained opulence. Note the way that
the simple canopy of white fabric provides a
refreshing foil to the dark wood tones of the
cathedral ceiling, creating a more private realm
within the expansive space.

# Design That Works from the Ground Up

**STATELY**
Like a canopy bed without the fuss, the simple yet stately design of the four-poster bed makes a strong but tasteful statement in any décor.

DIMENSIONS: H 30 IN. (76 CM) x D 19.75 IN. (50 CM) x W 21.75 IN. (55 CM)

## WHAT MAKES IT CLASSIC

- *CRAFTSMANSHIP AND QUALITY: Often crafted from solid mahogany and polished to a high gloss, antique four-poster beds are highly sought after. But thanks to quality manufacturers, accurate reproductions of eighteenth- and nineteenth-century designs are now available.*

- *AN EVOLVING STYLE: Modern four-poster beds are designed to fit most styles, from traditional American Colonial and Tudor styles to contemporary interpretations in metal, enamel, and brass. The clean lines of Shaker-inspired beds suit country and modern interiors with equal grace.*

- *NOBLE ORIGINS: During the sixteenth century, Dutch craftsmen were making many of Europe's most notable beds—among them classical four-posters—from ornately carved oak. Kings and nobles used their bedroom as a reception room, so their four-poster beds served as a sort of throne.*

Bedrooms are usually defined by relaxing, horizontal planes, with the bed as the centerpiece of it all. So how does one add drama and vertical height to a space without adding a bulky, large-scale piece such as an oversized armoire? Enter the four-poster bed, a tasteful bit of architecture that adds sophisticated elegance and interesting lines to any space.

### DETAILS THAT MAKE A DIFFERENCE

The four-poster concept is open to interpretation and has been adapted to virtually every kind of culture and climate throughout history. From simple, Shaker-inspired pencil-post versions to hand-turned examples carved with traditional motifs, there is a four-poster for every style and every space. The bed's elegant form and substantial dimensions lend a sense of definition to a wide-open space, making a four-poster bed an elegant addition to an expansive loft. With just a few alterations, the design can suit a variety of styles: With a patchwork quilt, a four-poster becomes wholly country, but when dressed in crisp cotton and flannel, it is quite masculine.

During the Middle Ages, when beds were designed for ceremonial appearances, the four posts supported a dramatic expanse of textiles. In the nineteenth-century, plantation owners in the hot, humid climates of the West Indies and the southern United States gravitated toward exposing the wood, and using the light, roughly made wooden frames to support practical canopies of thin, white mosquito netting.

< COUNTERPOINT
Tall, handsome posts combine with an ornate head- and footboard to give this rich mahogany bed a sense of regal importance. The bed's dark color provides a striking counterpoint to the room's gentle blue scheme, making it the focal point of this cozy bedroom.

# New Heights

For siblings sharing a room, bunk beds are an exciting option. The top bunk offers a new perspective and a certain cachet associated with being up higher than anyone else in the room. Yet the bottom bunk easily adapts into a private fort with the addition of a few strategically hung blankets.

**STACKABLE**
Often consisting of two separate, stackable units, these beds can be taken apart and used separately if preferred.

DIMENSIONS: L 79 IN. (201 CM) x W 41 IN. (104 CM) x H 71IN. (180 CM) IS AVERAGE

These are the beds that children fight over and that old soldiers look back on nostalgically as they recount their Army days. Of course, bunk beds need not be the spare, metal-frame models that hint of military barracks. With countless arrangements, materials, sizes, and shapes available today, there is a bunk bed for any room and almost any purpose.

## HOW TO USE THE AIR UP THERE

By raising one bed up off the ground, you can create space for lots of things beneath it. Among the most popular ways to utilize that space is, of course, the addition of a second bed. Traditional up-and-down models offer two twin-size beds, with a ladder providing access to the top bunk. Some models add further sleeping space by incorporating a full bed (or futon/frame combination) on the bottom, or even slipping a trundle beneath the bottom bunk.

### WHAT MAKES IT CLASSIC

- *GROWS WITH THE FAMILY: Most bunk beds can be separated into a two beds, making it easy to change a room around or divide the set to accommodate children moving into their own rooms.*

- *DESIGNER INTERPRETATIONS: The bunk bed is not limited in its look. It is produced in retro-styled iron beds, Mission-style versions from Stickley and others, and attractive painted-wood interpretations.*

- *AN INSTITUTIONAL CLASSIC: Commonly used in Army barracks and dormitories, bunk beds were created as a simple answer to a need for additional sleeping space. Many modern designs, usually executed in iron, speak to this institutional aesthetic—but in an attractive and charming way.*

But that reclaimed space is about more than just sleeping. Some sets place the bottom bunk perpendicular to the top, making room for a dresser, desk, or play area beneath. Still others eliminate the second bed altogether, and put the new alcove to use as a study or play area.

∧ VERSATILITY
Charming and practical, a pair of white oak bunk beds by Lexington offers versatility and style. Additional storage is provided by pull-out drawers beneath the bottom unit, and the beds can be easily separated into two twin beds.

∧ CONTEMPORARY

With its upright lines and right angles, this iron bed is a contemporary take on the classic form. It works equally well in modern, eclectic, and even country-style interiors.

< BALANCED

At once formal and whimsical, this ornate, asymmetrical iron bed is characterized by its unique headboard and the use of four different—yet perfectly balanced—finials. Perfect in an eclectic interior, this interesting design speaks to a variety of influences.

# Metal with a Touch of Grace

**REINTERPRETATIONS**
Whether scrolled or angular, modern foundries have revived the iron bed with faithful reproductions, retro-styled reinterpretations, and stunning new designs.

DIMENSIONS: W 54 IN. (137 CM) x L 77 IN. (196 CM) IS AVERAGE

How ironic that one of mankind's strongest materials should prove so pliable and graceful when placed in the hands of a skilled artisan. And while wrought-iron gates, screens, and sculpture all attest to the ironworker's craft, the medium takes on new dimensions when it becomes the basis for our most intimate furnishings. Combining cold, sturdy materials with soft down and warm blankets, the well-dressed iron bed is a study in contrasts.

## MINIMUM MATERIALS, MAXIMUM IMPACT
The strength of iron gives these beds their special talent: Only the thinnest lines are necessary to create a sturdy bed that will withstand years of use. As a result, an iron bed can make a strong statement without looking, well, huge. This makes it possible to place a grand bed, complete with a high, ornate headboard, in a fairly small space.

In a modern room, an antique iron bed adds an element of unexpected charm and warmth. Consider the way the vinelike black iron of an ornate headboard contrasts with the stark white walls of a minimalist loft, creating a work of graphic, three-dimensional art. In a country interior, a vintage institutional design—inspired by the hospital wards of the early 1900s and coated with crackle-glaze paint—provides an edgy counterpoint to natural beadboard wainscoting and gingham linens and curtains.

### WHAT MAKES IT CLASSIC

- *ATTRACTIVE AND FUNCTIONAL: The sturdiness of iron beds makes them a great investment— they'll withstand the punishment of children, as well as the grandchildren who inherit them. And with the exception of polishing any brass trim, they're virtually maintenance free.*

- *THE APPEAL OF AN ANTIQUE: The virtually indestructible nature of the material has allowed many of these period examples to survive, and vintage beds—from rare antiques to institutional models—remain relatively accessible. Built before the advent of queen- and king-size beds, these antique examples can be converted to larger sizes without sacrificing their authenticity.*

- *A PROUD HISTORY: Metal has been a common component in furniture for centuries; in fact, beds made partly or entirely of metal were found in the ruins of Pompeii, Italy.*

## INDUSTRIAL ART
Although earlier examples exist, iron beds truly came into fashion during the late eighteenth century, when the industrial revolution made iron a popular material for all kinds of furnishings as well as machinery. Early iron beds were handcrafted, one-of-a-kind originals; later beds were mass-produced. Reflecting different periods of design—from the classical forms of pre-Revolutionary France to hospital-issue models from the Depression-era United States—these beds suit any number of styles.

Anglepoise Lamp

Hansen Swing-Arm Lamp

Tizio Lamp

PH Series Lamps

Costanza Lamp

Brera Lamp

Bestlite Lamp

Berenice Lamp

Bauhaus Lamp

Akari Lamp

classic lighting

# A Lesson in Flexibility

**AUSTERE**

The original Bakelite-based Anglepoise boasts all the charm of any classic Deco piece. Simple and austere, it adds a touch of thirties class to even the most modern workstations.

DIMENSIONS: 29-IN. (74 CM) REACH, WITH 6-FT. (2 METER) CORD

## WHAT MAKES IT CLASSIC

- *A SUBTLE WORK OF ART: Simple, sturdy, and infinitely adaptable, the Anglepoise lamp is so perfect in its design that it's often overlooked. It has been endlessly imitated and reinterpreted, yet the design remains as fresh and useful today as it was when it was introduced in the thirties.*

- *AN INTEREST-ADDING ELEMENT: The Anglepoise's purposeful shape and clean lines work well in all sorts of settings, from a room filled with colors to a muted environment where pure geometry reigns. Although used primarily for task lighting, the Anglepoise only needs a simple adjustment to create a more general, ambient illumination.*

< INSPIRED

Executed in bright chrome, this modern take on the Anglepoise illuminates a the space with grace and ease. The Anglepoise's spring-tension arm, inspired by the human anatomy, offers perfect task illumination; its flexible arm allows for easy-to-position light.

The Anglepoise table lamp boils down functionality to its elegant best, and the number of times it has been imitated is testimony to its status as a true classic. The original was designed by George Cawardine and first produced in 1932. Pure functionality drove its design—this simple desk lamp offered adaptable, effective task lighting without taking up a great deal of surface space. Cawardine nurtured an interest in ergonomics and found inspiration for the Anglepoise in the human arm. His basic design—which uses springs as counterweights to keep the lamp's arm in the desired position—remains in production by Anglepoise and its countless imitators today. The very name has become the Xerox of the lighting world, and the word *anglepoise* is now used to describe any lamp based on Cawardine's original design.

Many imitations of the lamp have been quite successful. One of these is a Danish translation, the Luxo light, which Jacob Jacobsen began producing in 1937 when he acquired the Anglepoise patent. The appeal of the Danish version, like that of the original and other imitators, is simple: Put light where you need it, and minimize the mechanisms needed to get it there. It's one of those design solutions that are so effective they seem obvious.

## THE BEST OF PAST AND PRESENT

The original Anglepoise lamp consisted of a lacquered metal lamp atop a Bakelite base. Today, it is most often all metal and available in many colors. It can be purchased with a solid circular base or a screw clamp.

The lamp's pure attention to function makes the Anglepoise an extremely versatile piece. While it is most often used in a home office, it would fit equally well in a library, den, or living room. The simple, metal surfaces don't compete with deep, rich woods, and complement glass, metal, and other contemporary surfaces well. The classic Anglepoise acts as the perfect foil for a variety of decorating schemes. Its timeless design lends an air of industrial chic to rustic interiors and loans more modern surfaces, such as metal, Lucite, and glass, a bit of retro-infused warmth.

# The Chameleon of Lighting

Once you start looking for it, you notice that George Hansen's swing-arm lamp is everywhere. In homes, restaurants, hotels, and offices, this understated yet elegant lamp perches on tabletops, stands beside armchairs, and hangs mounted on walls. In every case it looks as though it were custom designed for that very spot, in that specific room.

The beauty of Hansen's design lies in the lamp's simple shape, timeless finish, and essential functionality. This lamp is meant to be noticed, but not necessarily noted. Its ageless style and simple design are almost always taken for granted: It is a dependable element for lighting and accessorizing virtually any space.

### THE LITTLE LAMP THAT COULD

When he set up shop in New York after the World War II, Hansen's goal was to make "utterly simple things"—among them, his elegant, highly functional lamps. Harry Hinson purchased Hansen's company in 1991, and Hinson & Company continues to sell some 5,000 swing-arm lamps each year. The lamps come in a range of finishes, including brass, steel, and gray or white enamel, and are available as desk lamps, table lamps, floor lamps, and wall-mounted fixtures. Over the past fifty years, designers and decorators have used each iteration widely in many types of environments.

The timeless appeal of the Hansen makes it an elegant addition to almost any setting, from traditional to contemporary. It works as task lighting on a desk, as a reading light beside a bed or comfy chair, or as a tasteful accent atop an antique table. In a formal living room, the wall-mounted version's diminutive shade and sleek arms offer a sense of luxury. In a family room, perched between an overstuffed sofa and a Stickley rocker, the freestanding floor lamp's simple shade and smooth arms act as grace notes.

## TRADITIONAL

The stately elegance of the Hansen swing-arm lamp works in virtually any design situation. A simple but hardworking design paired with a rich finish and a traditional silhouette make this the only lamp you'll ever need.

DIMENSIONS: H 34 IN. (86 CM) x D 19.5 IN. (50 CM) x W 16.5 IN. (42 CM)

## WHAT MAKES IT CLASSIC

- *UNIVERSAL STYLE: Finished in brass and topped with a simple paper shade, the Hansen swing-arm embodies classic beauty. It has an ageless grace that makes it hard to place in a historic context—it might have been designed in the twenties, fifties, or perhaps just this morning. For that reason, it works well in almost any design situation.*

- *CLARITY OF DESIGN: The Hansen has a stately presence that many lamps lack. But while it is indeed beautiful, it remains first and foremost a lamp; it asserts its identity clearly, then blends in with the background.*

- *CLARITY OF PURPOSE: Hansen was stationed in Labrador during World War II when he found himself wishing he could read in bed. He created the first version of his now-classic lamp out of copper tubing and a tin can. Schooled in physics and in art, Hansen had worked in antiques shops before the war, and his experience most certainly informed his purposeful design.*

∧ BEDSIDE ILLUMINATION

A pair of wall-mounted Hansen swing-arm lamps provide perfect bedside illumination in a room where space is at a premium. By keeping the lamps off the tables (and the tables off the floor), these homeowners have created an illusion of spaciousness and a sleek, minimalist aesthetic.

< BRIDGES THE GAP

Traditional furnishings and a formidable collection of artwork take center stage in this contemporary bedroom. The wall-mounted Hansen swing-arm lamp bridges the gap between table and wall, providing perfect reading light but little visual distraction.

< PERFECTLY AT HOME

Here, a Hansen swing-arm is perfectly at home amid charming country antiques. Again, it keeps the bedside table free of clutter, yet it seems as traditional as an old-fashioned bedside lamp.

∧ A CLASSIC
A classic among classics, the Tizio's pleasing
proportions are at home against a backdrop of
artifacts from the ancient world.

# The Most Famous Lamp in the World

**BLACK MATTE**
The absence of visible wiring and its unique counterweighted arm and adjustable glass-block head distinguish the Tizio, perhaps the most famous of all modern lighting fixtures. Made by Artemide, it is constructed of aluminum and thermoplastic with a black matte, lacquered finish.

DIMENSIONS: H 32 IN. (81 CM) TO 42 IN. (107 CM) X 4 IN. (11 CM) BASE

## WHAT MAKES IT CLASSIC

- *AN ENDURING AESTHETIC: Few designs of the seventies have managed to endure the way the Tizio has. Thirty years after its introduction, it continues to grace desks, drafting tables, and nightstands all over the world.*

- *THE BEST OF PAST AND PRESENT: Tizio is very much a product of its time. An expression of seventies technology, it is also a celebration of new halogen lighting technology.*

*GROUNDBREAKING DESIGN: The technology of this lamp may not be considered as state-of-the-art as when it was introduced in 1972, but its stunning architectural design is still regarded as cutting edge. Its unique, counterweighted arm and compact, glass-block head, combined with the absence of cumbersome wires, make it an elegant addition to virtually any interior.*

Richard Sapper's enigmatic Tizio lamp may be the most recognizable lamp in production. It is manufactured in Italy by Artemide. The company fondly calls it "the most famous lamp in the world," and, indeed, it has been illuminating interiors of all styles since it was introduced in 1972. The Tizio is at once a sample of fine engineering, a stunning architectural presence, and a useful business tool. It is also ergonomically correct.

Sapper eliminated the clunky tension springs that other desk lamps used to keep the lighting element in position and instead created a counterweight balance system with two arms. This design enabled him to minimize the weight and bulk of the object dramatically, while it offered the user the convenience of adjusting the light with a touch of the finger. Sapper also eliminated the bulky shades that characterized earlier lamps by using the tiny but powerful halogen bulbs that were then quite new to the market. In addition, its design was the first to use the arm structure itself as an electrical, low-voltage conductor. This innovation eliminated the cord that so often interferes with the appearance of other lamps.

### A MODERN MASTERPIECE
The Tizio lamp is one of those classic twentieth-century pieces that works well in almost any room, with almost any décor. Its straight lines, block base, and slightly arced weights are unmistakably contemporary. But the Zenlike sense of balance and minimalism that defines this light fixture help it to fit into a variety of environments.

Even in a room with rough-hewn walls and floors, these sleek pieces provide a contrast that is striking without being jarring. Don't confine them to the home office—these beautiful lamps provide superior illumination for bedside reading.

# Creating Layers of Light

The classics are often spartan in their simplicity, yet the clean lines and architectural shape of Poul Henningsen's deco-style PH Series lamps are defined by their complex combinations of louvers and light. The beauty of these fixtures lies in their sculptural form and thoughtful practicality. The shades (which are composed of separate pieces of lacquered copper and fitted together on a chromated steel frame) cover the bulb while directing light to the chosen surface. The result is diffused light with minimal contrast between the surfaces. This award-winning design makes these lamps marvelously multifunctional, providing both direct and ambient light.

The original, legendary, three-shaded lamp was the impetus for an entire line now known as the PH Series. Today, manufacturer Louis Poulsen offers a PH-inspired lamp for every décor and every purpose.

**UNIQUE MARRIAGE**
PH's classic Artichoke fixture represents a unique marriage of industrial materials and organic form. The best feature of the Artichoke—and all the lamps in the PH Series—is the way that they break the light into soft, many-textured layers.

DIMENSIONS: VARY

They are available as pendants and table lamps. The 1958 variation, sometimes called the Artichoke, is composed of multiple pieces of metal, each positioned to direct light and mask glare. In some of the later versions, the tonal effect was subtly varied by adding color to the interior of the lamps.

**BEAUTIFUL LIGHTING THAT WORKS**
The strong, horizontal lines, industrial materials, and functional illumination make the pendants a natural choice almost any setting, especially the kitchen or home office. There, the sophisticated elemental shape of the lamps adds visual interest yet still emphasizes simplicity and effectiveness. The desk lamp, too, is a sculptural gem that delivers its light with subtle precision and fits with contemporary or traditional accessories equally comfortably.

**WHAT MAKES IT CLASSIC**

- *FOR ANY SETTING: The myriad PH Series lamps offer superior lighting for large areas, making them popular choices for commercial spaces such as libraries and restaurants. At home, they work exceptionally anywhere that general lighting is needed and artistry is appreciated.*

- *LIGHT FOR LIGHT'S SAKE: Designers note that the best feature of the PH Series may not be the fixture at all, but the light emitted. Charlie Lazor, of Minneapolis-based Blu Dot, notes "They control and shed light very carefully, almost architecturally.... Most lighting is a bulb and then something over it, a shade or a globe. The PH lamps break up the light into layers, and that's what makes them exceptional,"*

- *A PROUD HISTORY: The PH Series was based on Henningsen's rigorous analysis of a lamp shade's function, shape, and size and was inspired by the soft glow of the petroleum lamps with which he'd grown up.*

The more dramatic, multilayered Artichoke lamps provide a stronger statement in an entry or formal dining room. The unique design of this PH's louvered shade breaks the light into layers, creating interesting illumination throughout the area. These remnants of the Jazz Age add a retro flavor to contemporary interiors.

∧ STUNNING FIXTURES

Large-scale Poulsen lamps offer all the drama of chandeliers in this spacious banquet room, but without the stuffy, overly formal feel of old-fashioned crystal. These stunning fixtures provide a soft glow and add architectural interest, while the repetition of the form results in a calm rhythm throughout the hall.

< SOFT GLOW

Taking on a decidedly Eastern flavor, a pair of PH Series pendants illuminates a sleek, modern dining area. The soft glow of the dish-like fixtures lends warmth and interest to the sparse décor without disturbing the calmness of the atmosphere.

< SYMMETRY

The striking horizontal lines of this PH Series lamp lend a Prairie-style sense of symmetry to this cozy breakfast nook. Multipaned windows, vintage seating, and charming beadboard paneling work in perfect harmony with the deco-edged lighting fixture.

∧ SLEEK VERTICAL
A design standard in the hotels of Europe, the Costanza lamp complements clean, modern interiors with its sleek, vertical lines and tradition-inspired polycarbonate shade. The shade's filtering qualities combined with the lamp's dimmer feature ensure that the fixture can provide the perfect lighting for any situation.

< ARCHITECTURAL INTEREST
In a modern bedroom, the subtle shape of Costanza provides the perfect bedside lighting, while offering a bit of architectural interest to a room filled with low furniture. Without straying too far from our accepted understanding of what a lamp looks like, the Costanza manages to be at once comfortable and unexpectedly fresh.

# The Only Lamp You'll Ever Need

**SLENDER**
Sleek yet subtle, contemporary without straying too far from tradition, the Costanza lamp is a classic for every style and season. A mere touch of the slender wand turns the light on and off.

DIMENSIONS: DESK LAMP: H 20 IN. (51CM); 5-IN. (12.7 CM) BASE; 10-IN. (25.5 CM) SHADE

## WHAT MAKES IT CLASSIC

- *USEFUL DESIGN: The Costanza's uncomplicated stem and clean, elegant shade deliver functionality as well as style. The silkscreened shades offer soft, diffused light, while the dimmer feature adds versatility and adaptability. As a result, the lighting provided is as much a feature as the design of the lamp itself.*

- *VERSATILE BEAUTY: The Costanza is available in anodized black or bright, natural aluminum, with shades silkscreened in any of a number of colors. And with three formats to choose from—a fixed-height table lamp (its original iteration), a floor lamp, or with a telescoping stem for adjustable lighting—there truly is a Costanza for every situation and décor.*

- *A DESIGNER'S STANDBY: Dutch lighting designer Rogier van Heide sings the praises of the Costanza, calling it "the archetypal floor fixture." He notes that its minimalistic, contemporary style suits virtually any interior.*

When you have a room that calls for a simple, classic lamp with a dash of quirky personality, turn to the classic Costanza. This lamp's contemporary and whimsical take on conventional design help it to keep up with the rigors of sleek modernism, but it is even more at home in a room where eclecticism rules. Simple lines and elegant forms provide a surprisingly harmonious contrast with pine floors or an antique table or desk. The Costanza adopts a minimalist approach to the traditional silhouette, and as a result, this spartan piece provides the perfect finishing touch to any décor.

Contemporary yet classic, modern without looking space age, the Costanza lamp fits into virtually any room. It is equally at home on a country pine desk, a mahogany library table, or a modern, glass-topped work surface. It works beside a sleek leather sofa, next to an antique iron bed, or alongside an overstuffed Chippendale armchair. Available in two finishes and a variety of sizes as either a tabletop or floor lamp, the Costanza is one of the most versatile lighting designs ever produced.

## STYLE BY DESIGN

Designed by Paolo Rizzatto in 1986, the Costanza is a slim, elegant, and utterly simple reinterpretation of the standard table lamp and shade. A thin square of aluminum forms the lamp's base, into which is screwed a slender aluminum tube. The tube conceals the cord and supports the fiberglass-reinforced, polycarbonate shade. The dimmer switch is a sleek aluminum lever that extends from the primary stem at a 45-degree angle and allows one to adjust the light level with a simple touch.

Rizzatto updated the classic lampshade by using polycarbonate, a new material at the time used primarily for creating automobile dashboards. Silkscreened in any one of several colors with added texture, Rizzatto's design diffuses a soft light similar to that which is transmitted through rice-paper shades. It's a look that is comforting and soothing, yet thoroughly modern and always interesting.

**SOFT ILLUMINATION**
The award-winning Brera pendant lamp is an effective lighting element with the heart of a poet. The opal-white glass diffuser provides soft illumination, while the organic form and cool, soothing texture generate an overall sense of calm.

DIMENSIONS: H 11 IN. (27.9 CM) x W 6 IN. 15 CM; 16-FT (4.8-METER) CORD

**WHAT MAKES IT CLASSIC**

- *A MODERN JEWEL: The Brera has all the timeless sophistication and wearability of a string of pearls. Its defining features—a simple shape, an interesting finish, and an unobtrusive elegance—make it the essential accessory for any home-design wardrobe.*

- *ARTISTIC INSPIRATION: According to Castiglioni, the Brera was inspired by a painting at the Pinacoteca di Brera in Milan, Piero della Francesca's altar painting* The Madonna and Child with Federico da Montefeltro. *The scene depicted includes an ostrich egg—symbolic of the Virgin Birth— which inspired Castiglioni's now-classic design.*

> EARTHY
The sweeping curves of a stairway and the geometric shape of a doorway meet beneath the earthy illumination of a Brera ceiling fixture. This is a lamp that manages to be modern and subtly retro at the same time.

# The Shape of Light

The simple, glowing form of the classic Brera lamp does much more than merely facilitate the distribution of light—it is the shape of light itself. The egg-shaped fixtures incorporate a few carefully chosen, decidedly man-made materials—acid-treated glass, steel, and plastic—in an organic form that is thoroughly modern, yet utterly timeless. Brera's egg-shaped glass diffuser is split in two parts held together by a ring nut that provides accessibility to the bulb. The lamp, available as a standing floor lamp, a hanging pendant, or a wall lamp, adds a soft, glowing, ambient light to almost any setting.

Achille Castiglioni designed the Brera for Flos in 1992, when he was 74 years old. The lamp's continued popularity testifies to the designer's long career and copious talent. The spare profile gives Brera a sleek, contemporary feel, but like any classic, the lamp's form is timeless and suited to any number of design schemes.

## BEYOND MODERN
The style and sophisticated charm of the Brera shine in modern settings, but this unique fixture's simple silhouette and soft, diffused glow lend themselves to a variety of less obvious design situations as well. A pair of Brera pendant lamps could light either a contemporary black lacquer table or a more traditional oak dining set with equal grace and poise. Similarly, the floor model could no doubt be found in a sleek and minimalist living room, but it also could provide soft, ambient light amidst the leather reading chairs and stacks of bookcases in a lavish, snug library.

A natural for the stark white and steel scheme of a modern loft or gallery-style space, Brera offers a soothing shape and calm glow that also make a beautiful statement when paired with contrasting textures and colors. Beside an opulent sofa upholstered in rich red damask, the floor lamp provides an elegant juxtaposition in both feel and form. Walls and ceilings of cool cobalt or navy blue become vibrant backdrops for the elegant pendant lamps. Hung above a Victorian sideboard or placed beside a classic Morris chair, the Brera punctuates an eclectic décor, adding modern interest and elegant illumination.

∧ BALANCING

The Bestlite pillar lamp, with its extending arm,
is a perfect lighting option for the bedside area.
The wall-mounted fixture adds visual interest
above the sleeping space, balancing the soft horizontal lines that characterize most bedrooms
with a harder texture and touch of height.

**BAUHAUS**
Executed in aluminum and steel, the Bauhaus-influenced Bestlite table lamp has been in continuous production since 1930.

DIMENSIONS: H 34 IN. (85.3 CM)

## WHAT MAKES IT CLASSIC

- *A WORK OF ART THAT REALLY WORKS: The flexible arm makes it easy to focus the light exactly where you want it, making it a natural for desks and bedside tables. But what serves as a perfectly efficient task or reading light during the workday can be easily transformed into attractive accent lighting when night falls.*

- *MATERIALS AND CRAFTSMANSHIP: The Bestlite is known for its superior craftsmanship as well as its attractive lines and its attention to function. The lamp's manufacturer, Best & Lloyd (a Birmingham firm established in 1840), has a long-standing reputation for high-quality manufacturing standards, which has almost certainly contributed to the lamp's enduring popularity.*

- *AN ACCESSIBLE TREASURE: The Bauhaus-influenced Bestlite is part of London's Design Museum collection, as well as many other museum collections. It has been in continuous production since its creation and has been a design standard for more than seventy years.*

# Seamless Functionality

Rarely do functionality, aesthetic appeal, and engineering genius come together as seamlessly as they do in Robert Dudley Best's stunning Bestlite. Excellent materials and workmanship and a variety of useful forms make this little gem perfect for almost any room. Designed by Best in 1930, the simple yet evocative Bestlite displays the influence of the Bauhaus movement and the 1925 International Exhibition of Modern and Industrial Arts. The task light's spun aluminum head and aluminum and steel arm represent the clarity of purpose and elegant approach to functionality that the Bauhaus designers promulgated.

### EASY ADAPTABILITY

The practical beauty of the Bestlite lies in its universal movements. The shade rotates and tilts, the arm tilts up and down, and the clutch assembly both rotates around its pillar and slides up and down. All models are available with a chromium, polished brass, or matte nickel finish. Shades, base covers, fixing brackets, and slider support tube knobs are available in a range of colors. The culmination of these unique features is a series of lamps that is infinitely adaptable and always appropriate.

The fluid movement of the arching arm makes the Bestlite a work of art in and of itself. The smooth, spun-aluminum shade and sturdy yet adaptable stem speak to the lamp's Bauhaus influences. This is the perfect desk lamp, offering superior illumination while sacrificing only a minimum of desk space.

The Bestlite family has a lamp for every space. The freestanding floor lamp has a fully adjustable arm and shade; a cantilever version of the floor lamp has a counterbalanced arm that pivots for extra height and projection. Either model makes a great accent for a living room or parlor, where the substantial, angled shade really holds its own amongst lush, upholstered pieces. The table lamp works for bedside or office, and the wall-mount versions can work virtually anywhere. Even in the kitchen, this workhorse puts function first and yet still manages to contribute to the overall composition of the room.

# A Dainty Light That Works Hard

## SOPHISTICATED

The Berenice is the epitome of modern design, combining form and function in a single elegant piece. Available in black or silver steel with a glass diffuser shade that comes in green, blue, black, or silver, this slim yet powerful light is as versatile as it is sophisticated.

DIMENSIONS: H 34 IN. (86.4 CM) (FULLY EXTENDED); W 17 IN. (43.2 CM) (EXTENSION FROM JOINT); 5-IN. (12.7-CM) BASE

## WHAT MAKES IT CLASSIC

- *A DESIGN THAT WORKS: Berenice's sophisticated form has been accepted into the design collections of several museums around the world.*

- *A VERSATILE FORM: The arm of the Berenice lamp is fully articulated, balanced, and adjustable and is anchored to a weighted base that can be freestanding, fastened to a desk or other piece of furniture, or mounted on a wall. This makes it a perfect choice when surface space is tight or in design schemes that emphasize clutter-free surfaces.*

- *ACCESSIBLY ARTISTIC: It is not price, of course, but design that determine popularity. Luceplan's (Berenice's manufacturer) leaders hold this idea dear and strive to keep their quality designs relatively affordable, even after they've entered the realm of classics.*

Architectural yet dainty, sweet yet powerful, Berenice is the grande dame of modern lighting design masquerading as the ingénue. The thin, spare lines and charming colored glass "hat" that define this stunning fixture might seem fragile at first glance, but this is one hardworking lamp. With a fully articulated arm and a 35-watt halogen bulb that provides the most direct, color-pure task lighting currently available, Berenice does her job beautifully, and looks beautiful doing it.

The slender, elegant Berenice is a complex and flexible product with a poetic simplicity. Instead of leaving exposed cords, the designers chose to run power through the lamp's arms. And the colored glass shade produces a gentle sparkle that makes this lamp as much a design element as it is an efficient tool for lighting a work area.

The lamp's malleability lends it an almost flirtatious appeal. Up close, it's easy to see the precise detailing and meticulously refined joinery between components. Alberto Meda (who, along with Paolo Rizzatto, designed the lamp in 1985) is known for his minimal use of materials, and that approach is evident in the slim Berenice. His interest in transparency also is expressed in the blue and green diffuser shades that seem to glow when the lamp is lit.

### A TOOL FOR DECORATING

The Berenice is a task light with a great deal more personality than one might expect from this type of lamp. While its superior illumination and sleek design make it a natural for the office, Berenice's slim profile render it a perfect option for any spot in which one might want to curl up with a book. You can use a Berenice with all sorts of pieces and in all sorts of places. The design is contemporary, but is surprisingly at home amidst woods, rich colors, and fabrics. Two Berenice lamps flanking a bed produce opposing angles that provide a whimsical accent in any bedroom. In a living room or study, Berenice's slim, metallic form is a wonderful foil to over-stuffed, upholstered furniture.

∧ SOFTLY ECHOES
Used here as a bedside lamp, a Berenice provides ample overhead lighting for bedtime readers without disrupting the open, airy atmosphere of this seaside home. The thin steel form of the lamp softly echoes the heavy, black window frames, further emphasizing the wide ocean views beyond the panes.

< ADDS MOTION
The Berenice's spare form leaves lots of space for objets d'art in this eclectic living room. Paintings and pottery take center stage alongside the soft upholstered couch; the lamp's long, lean profile adds motion to the tabletop vignette without being distracting. Note how the Berenice's glowing blue shade highlights the intense colors of the painting behind the sofa.

< CAREFUL BLEND
The restful atmosphere of this quiet bedroom results from a careful blend of textures and forms. Warm wood floors, soft textiles, and spare walls lay the foundation for an eclectic blend of Eastern and Scandinavian influences, while the more modern table, chairs, and Berenice lamp add a postindustrial punch.

# Form follows Function, Beautifully

**INHERENTLY APPEALING**
The Bauhaus table lamp, sometimes called the WG 24, is the essence of Bauhaus style. Superior craftsmanship, incomparable materials, and a clean, functional, and inherently appealing design define this classic piece.

DIMENSIONS: H 14 IN. (35.6 CM) X W 7 IN. (17.8 CM)

## WHAT MAKES IT CLASSIC

- *AN ARTISTIC STATEMENT: Rarely does a function-first design take one's breath away the way that the Bauhaus lamp does. True to its inspiration, it is functional and sensible. But the layering of contrasting materials and the strong silhouette make this piece truly stunning.*

- *A GENUINE PIECE OF HISTORY: The Bauhaus school was a social movement as well as an artistic one. It advocated cooperation among craftsmen and the elevation of the status of "ordinary" objects. This lamp, a work of supreme craftsmanship and beauty, answers both objectives.*

- *THE CROSSROADS OF DESIGN: The Bauhaus table lamp, designed by Wilhelm Wagenfeld and Karl J. Jucker in 1924, offers a distinct departure from the ornate styles typically produced at that time, yet embraces some of the materials—including clear and opaline glass—that typify elements of other contemporary stylistic movements.*

The Bauhaus lamp is the antithesis of the ornate, historically bound designs that the Bauhaus school sought to replace. Considered by many to be one of the first lamps of modern design, this lamp is so perfect in form that it has long outlasted the school of thought that provided its inspiration. Its purposeful design and balanced proportions give it a strong presence that does not overpower other elements in the room. The soft illumination of the opaline glass infuses rooms with a soothing glow.

## MATERIALS THAT APPEAL TO THE SENSES
This lamp has a plain but elegant industrial look that epitomizes the aesthetic of the Bauhaus school. Its glass shade echoes the basic lighting components found in European factories in the twenties. The opaline globe sits on a glass column and base; a metal tube within the column unobtrusively delivers power to the bulb inside the globe. The metal components are nickel-plated and glossy. This lamp gains its classic appeal and decorating versatility from its honest and direct use of materials.

Perhaps because it's an "old" contemporary design, this lamp benefits greatly from being juxtaposed with humble materials and forms. The mixing of styles that has been gaining popularity in recent years has revealed the beauty of pieces such as this one to those who might have shied away from its modern associations. You don't need a white room and glass coffee table to use the Bauhaus lamp; a backdrop of exposed brick and wide-plank pine floors will serve just as well, if not better.

< COMFORTABLE GLOW
Unlike many modern lamps, the Bauhaus table lamp is contemporary without being cold. In a bedroom, the calm, mushroom-like shape adds a soft, comfortable glow. The blend of nickel with clear and opaline glass works well with a variety of textures; here, it echoes the metal hardware on the nightstands while providing a gentle contrast with the wood furniture and floor.

# Weightless Light

## LIGHT SCULPTURES

The Japanese word *akari* refers to light in the form of illumination and relates to the concept of weightlessness. The Akari lamps are a testament to both senses of the word. Since 1951, these biomorphic light sculptures have been made by the Ozeki Company in Gifu, Japan.

DIMENSIONS: VARY FOR COLUMN LAMP, H 74 IN. (188 CM) X W 18 IN. (45.7 CM)

## WHAT MAKES IT CLASSIC

- *ACCENT LIGHTING AND MORE: Adding an Akari lamp provides a room with instant character. They illuminate in such a way that the entire space seems to have been conceived and executed by a lighting designer, while the sculptural form adds interest to even the sparest of spaces.*

- *FORM PLUS FUNCTION: Designer Charlie Lazor says that the Akari is unique in that it provides more light than you expect. "Often, you go to buy a lamp, and then you realize that it provides only accent lighting. You cannot read by it or have it light even half a room," he says. "The Akari lamps actually do provide strong light, and they do the job in a great, special, Noguchi way."*

- *ENDURING ORIGINALITY: Noguchi hoped that "originality might survive mass production," and many of his enduring designs helped ensure that it would.*

The Akari freeform lamps bring a sense of whimsy and softness into the spaces they inhabit, and they do it with a cool, comfortable glow that few lamps can replicate. In a setting characterized by sleek lines and contemporary pieces, they help mitigate the rigidity that sometimes infects modern environments. And while they probably won't work with chintz, they do lend a touch of adventure to more traditional settings.

Sculptor and designer Isamu Noguchi was inspired by the bamboo-skeleton lanterns created in Gifu, Japan. While visiting the city after World War II, he was invited by the mayor to create a contemporary lamp with these same materials. The result was the first Akari lamp, a sculptural masterpiece made of Gifu's signature washi paper—a unique substance made from mulberry bark—stretched over a frame of higo bamboo ribbing.

### OF POETRY AND WHIMSY

The long-standing appeal of Noguchi's well-crafted Akari lamps is attributed in part to the fact that they are, well, fun. They speak of delight. The lines, somehow inexact, speak directly to Noguchi's striving for an "imperfect" beauty and set the lamps apart from many other precise, clean-line classics. The table and floor lamps come in many forms, ranging from bulbous beehive shapes to elegant columns.

The bright illumination of an Akari makes it a perfect choice for an interior where the palette is dark but the mood is light. A backdrop of rich-hued paint, dark velvet curtains, or even exposed brick becomes a lesson in stunning contrasts when paired with a bright Akari table or floor lamp. And while the design itself is modern, its roots in a traditional Japanese form make it suitable for a variety of more old-fashioned interiors as well: Just as the Victorians were fascinated by the exotic fabrics and china patterns of the East, so too can an antique mahogany table enjoy the company of Noguchi's timeless masterpiece.

< SUBTLE

A pair of Akari lamps flanks an industrial book cart in the entryway of this home office. The subtle illumination and freeform shapes loan the sterile industrial furniture a sense of comfort and fun.

< STARK WHITE FINISH

The unusual shape of an Akari floor lamp plays off of the repetitious columns that define this loft-style space. The lamp complements the garden-styled furnishings it accompanies, and its stark white finish dramatically contrasts with the dark hardwood floors.

Town and Country Salt and Pepper Shakers

Ingegard Raman Decanter and Drinking Glass

Round-Up Storage System

Atomic Wall Clock

Hellerware

Eames Hang-It-All Coatrack

Eames Storage Unit

Cross Cabinet

Eames Folding Screen

Savoy Vase

classic storage & accessories

# Mundane Goes Modern

**CHARMING SHAKERS**
The undeniable stars of Eva Zeisel's charming Town and Country tableware collection, these charming shakers work with all sorts of dishes—and they're available in an array of bold colors.

DIMENSIONS: N/A

## WHAT MAKES IT CLASSIC

- *MORE THAN SHAKERS: There is an entire line of Town and Country ceramics to keep the salt and pepper company. Consider Zeisel's cruet set, a pair of intertwining vessels with cork stoppers that echo the design of the shakers. Display them together for an interesting interplay of related forms.*

- *POPULAR THEN AND NOW: Originally produced in the mid-forties by Red Wing Pottery of Minnesota, Zeisel's dinnerware became tabletop staples for America's modern design cognoscenti. The design has remained extremely popular, and reissues of her classic designs are now available from the Metropolitan Museum of Art.*

- *A PERSONAL DESIGN APPROACH: Departing from the functionalist, geometry-obsessed designs of her colleagues, Zeisel took her work in a decidedly more personal direction, noting, "Lines and form ...[should] express the designer's mood and his sense of humor."*

Some of the most striking home accessories combine high art with everyday function. The sculptural shapes and bold colors that are the hallmark of Eva Zeisel's 1946 Town and Country ceramic tableware make an expressive addition to any kitchen or casual dining area. Even without the matching plates, bowls, or serving pieces, these anthropomorphic salt and pepper shakers stand on their own to add a delightful element to any table setting.

### A MIX OF SENSIBILITIES

The appeal of Zeisel's design lies in its simplicity and adherence to the designer's abstract yet playful sensibilities. Monochromatic and devoid of ornament, the forms speak to our primal senses: the smooth lines and cool surfaces make them pleasing to hold, while their rich hues offer visual interest. These endearing ceramic shaker—with their mismatched sizes and intertwining necks—create a playful vignette on any tabletop. The simple pair, joined in a timeless embrace, makes an artful statement in a spot where a traditional set of shakers would go largely unnoticed.

And with countless colors available—from the nine original colors to the many additional ones added in several reissues of the pattern—collecting original and revival shakers can become a passion that takes them out of the kitchen and into the rest of the home. Consider the impact of a dozen or so of these shakers, in a rainbow of colors, arranged on an étagère. Alternatively, a parade of shakers uniform in color and size can add interest along a windowsill or marching across a narrow, wall-mounted shelf.

∧ SCULPTURAL FORM
In a simple yet elegant dining area, the organic
forms of Eva Zeisel's 1946 Town and Country
tableware make a statement. Here, the black-
and-white salt and pepper shakers stand out
against the natural wood of the tabletop and
chairs. Their sculptural form—almost ergonomic
in shape—is delightful.

## PURPOSEFUL DESIGN
Pure, clear glass and a dignified, purposeful design meet in this simple and charming decanter and drinking glass set designed by Ingegard Raman.

DIMENSIONS: H 30 IN. (76 CM) X D 19.75 IN. (50 CM) X W 21.75 IN. (55 CM)

## WHAT MAKES IT CLASSIC

- *MULTIPURPOSE: Use the Tanteralla at the bedside for a midnight drink of water, on the dinner table as a wine decanter, or on the bar to hold a rich, amber-colored sherry.*

- *OBJET D'ART: Sculptural form reveals a simple beauty treasured for items that are in daily use.*

- *ALWAYS STYLISH: Simple designs of good quality never go out of style. The Tanteralla makes for a beautiful wedding, anniversary, or housewarming gift that, due to its simplicity, will fit into anyone's décor.*

< ATTRACTIVE ACCESSORY
The simple forms of Ingegard Raman's decanter and drinking glass makes the set an attractive accessory on any table top. The clear glass emphasizes the decanter's contents— be it crystal-clear spring water or red wine.

# Beauty You Can Use

When can a utilitarian object be deemed a classic? When its inherent beauty and design elevate it beyond its designated function. The Ingegard Raman decanter and drinking glass—designed by one of the world's greatest living glass designers—are two such objects. The elegant shape is as well-suited to a bedside table for quenching late-night thirsts as it is to a shelf for display. "I never design anything I would not use myself," declares Raman.

## HALF EMPTY, HALF FULL
They possess a simple form and superior practicality that fits into any décor, and they serve their purpose with style. The elegant Tanteralla, produced by Orrefors, and earlier designs produced by Skrufs, takes the simple act of a drinking a glass of water—or any other beverage—to the level of high art.

Even empty, the decanter's pure form reveals a simple beauty. Display it on a shelf or tabletop with other glass vessels or decanters in different sizes and materials.

The Tanteralla decanter and drinking glass build on a similar product Raman produced for Skrufs in 1968. The newer one is laced with a tribute to Simon Gate and Edward Hald, pioneers of Orrefors design. "My work is always a link between simplicity, function, and aesthetic values," Raman sums up. "There's something about the interplay between the strength and fragility of glass that compels me. It's a magical medium. Nothing else has this transparency."

# A Mod Take on Modular

Who would have thought that rounding the corners of a stackable storage system would create such a flurry of excitement? That's exactly what happened when Italian designer Anna Castelli Ferrieri debuted her Round-Up storage system in the late sixties. Flexible, fun, and oh-so-groovy, Ferrieri's functional units pack modern impact while packing away the stuff.

## MODERN MATERIAL, MODERN DESIGN

The first furniture to be fashioned of injection-molded ABS, a shiny but bendable plastic, Ferrieri's storage system, suitable for the bedroom, bathroom, office, kitchen, family room, or nursery, was an instant hit when it was introduced. Its compelling form, practically unlimited stackability and reasonable price made these little units a must-have accessory. Aside from being able to put things into them, owners could sit on them, have tea on them, and wheel them around the room.

Their shape and endless functionality makes these little bins as desirable today as they were some forty years ago. The Round-Up bins in singles or multiples can be used to hold office supplies, dry goods in the kitchen, toys in the nursery, or books by your bed. Stacked in a corner in a living room or family room, a few units provide a tidy hideaway for newspapers and magazines, and can be used as seating when needed. In a bathroom, they keep towels, shampoo bottles, and medicines dust free and out of sight.

## ENDLESS FLEXIBILITY

In production since 1969, Anna Castelli Ferrieri's Round-Up storage units offer endless flexibility in a fun, modular form. They can be used in any room in the house, and moved around as storage needs change.

DIMENSIONS VARY: TWO-COMPARTMENT AVERAGE IS H 16 IN. (40 CM) X D 13 IN. (32 CM); THREE-COMPARTMENT AVERAGE IS H 23 IN. (58 CM) X D 13 IN. (32 CM)

## WHAT MAKES IT CLASSIC

- *FORWARD-THINKING FORM: Constructed of maintenance-free and virtually indestructible ABS plastic, the units are also a no-brainer to put together—they require no tools or screws of any kind, they just stack.*

- *FLEXIBLE FUNCTION: As single units, or stacked in groups of four, five, or more, the Round-Up system can be used in an endless variety of arrangements to serve infinite functions. A collection of the containers can be used in one room or strewn about several rooms, and the arrangement can be changed and expanded to suit the evolving needs of the household.*

- *A MOD MASTERPIECE: First produced in the sixties, the Round-Up system has since become part of the permanent collection at the Museum of Modern Art, New York. The system continues to be produced by Kartell, the Milan-based plasticware firm for which Ferrieri originally designed the units.*

∧ ARCHITECTURAL FEATURE
Stacked in towers of varying heights, a collection of Round-Up storage units in bold colors becomes an architectural feature in this stark, white environment. While providing a useful system for stowing endless clutter, the units create a skyline of surfaces upon which lamps and collectibles can be displayed.

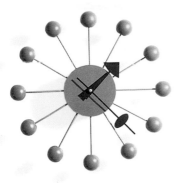

# Crazy for Chemistry

## MATTER AND SHADOW

Available in a number of colors and styles, the atomic wall clock is a treat for the eyes and a nice touch of three-dimensional art for any wall. Alone, they create an interesting pattern of matter and shadow; group a few of them together for an even more striking effect.

DIMENSIONS: D 18 IN. (46 CM) IS AVERAGE

## WHAT MAKES IT CLASSIC

■ *A RETRO REVIVAL: Out of production for twenty years, this is a design whose time has come again. Now produced for the mass market, it is available from the Vitra Design Museum Collection.*

■ *A TASTE OF EISENHOWER-ERA OPTIMISM: Informed by the cheerful yet naive outlook of the atomic age, Nelson's clocks speak to a particular point in American history. Nostalgia for those less cynical times has increased the clock's appeal with designers and collectors alike.*

■ *LITTLE MATERIAL, BIG IMPACT: Nelson was one of the nation's earliest proponents of environmentalism. His clocks follow through on his philosophy of "doing more with less"— they create a striking statement with very little mass.*

< NUCLEAR-AGE EXCITEMENT
Alongside a curio filled with relics of postwar America, from vintage cameras to deco vases, the atomic wall clock provides an element of nuclear-age excitement. A Saarinen dinette finishes out the room.

Few home furnishings speak to the sensibilities of postwar Americans with the kind of succinct charm that characterizes George Nelson's series of late-forties clocks. Using the familiar balls and rods of chemistry, Nelson's series for the Howard Miller Clock Company prefigured the obsession with the atomic age that took root in America during the following decade. Managing at once to be both original and familiar, the design looks fresh and new, yet chances are, your parents had one hanging on their kitchen wall.

Taking on either star or spokelike shapes, the clocks are a design element in their own right, whether painted in bright orange or baby blue, rendered in simple stained wood or multihued.

## WALL ART IN THREE DIMENSIONS

Made of wood and metal, the clocks add fun and elegance to practically any interior, whether midcentury or contemporary. With their combination of round and linear forms, they are as much about sculpture and texture as they are about offering the time. These retro charmers look great in a living room, where their exuberant form lends fun and movement to the steady curves of upholstered furniture. The spoked design can spice up a kitchen wall, while the multicolored version makes a chic yet accessible addition to a child's bedroom or play space.

With several compelling designs and color combinations to choose from, it's hard to pick just one. Happily, they look great grouped—buy a few and keep track of the time in your three favorite cities.

# Plastic Plates for the Nobility

## UTTERLY SIMPLE

Stackable, practical, and utterly simple, Hellerware was ubiquitous in the seventies, the first choice in casual dinnerware for countless families. While other tableware has come and gone, Hellerware has remained in continuous production since it was introduced.

DIMENSIONS: DINNER PLATE: D 10 IN. (25 CM);
SOUP BOWL: D 5 IN. (13 CM) x H 2 IN. (6 CM);
SALAD PLATE: D 7 IN. (19 CM);
MUG: D 3 IN. (8 CM) x H 4 IN. (10 CM)

## WHAT MAKES IT CLASSIC

■ *CLEAN LINES, COOL MATERIAL: With its modular lines and durable melamine surface, Hellerware challenged the formality of fancy, fragile china and the cold earthiness of stoneware.*

■ *THE CUPS YOU GREW UP WITH: Practical and stylish, Hellerware was a popular dinnerware of the seventies, and it has been in continuous production since 1970.*

■ *LONGEVITY AND AVAILABILITY: Originally produced in 1964 under the name Compact by Articoli Plastici Elettrici in Milan, Alan Heller bought the original molds from Milan-based Articoli to produce Hellerware after production of the design in Italy ceased in 1970. Massimo and his wife and partner Leila Vignelli revisited the design after it was brought to the United States, adding coordinating cups, mugs, and a pitcher to the service.*

Simple, stackable, and virtually indestructible, the clever design of Hellerware dinnerware makes it the perfect solution for everyday dining. Inspired by modular furniture, these stylish and durable melamine dishes, bowls, and cups combine designer aesthetics with functionality. Awarded the vaunted Italian Compasso d'Oro prize the same year it was introduced, the practical tableware made of pedestrian plastic was singled out by the jury for the "nobility" of its design.

The hardy, minimalist dishes—designed by Massimo Vignelli—go from cupboard to table to dishwasher with ease and defy even the most destructive infants to dent their smooth contours. Only 10 inches (25 cm) in diameter, the dinner plates are nonetheless capacious, as are the system's bowls and cups. Molded with a deep lip that helps keep food on the plate and allows for easy nesting, Hellerware stores in satisfying stacks, making it the perfect second set of dishes for cramped urban dwellers.

## A CLASSIC THAT'S AT HOME ANYWHERE

Incorporating these classic shapes into a contemporary home is virtually effortless—the pragmatic design serves the needs of casual dining service gracefully in just about any setting. They are child friendly, and their stark, smooth profiles add a freshness to casual dinner settings. The perfect solution for outdoor dining, picnics, and barbecues, Hellerware is stylish dinnerware meant to be used and enjoyed on a regular basis.

∧ INDESTRUCTIBLE
Tidy stacks of Hellerware fill an open cabinet in
this mod apartment. Virtually indestructible and
easy to store, these plates are a wonderful solution for everyday dining and a popular choice for
urban dwellers short on storage space.

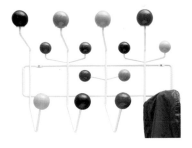

# A Colorful Storage Solution

With its white powder-coated wire frame and painted ball hooks in nine candy colors, the Eames Hang-It-All is a cheerful alternative to vanilla-flavored coatracks. Used well beyond the children's room in modern design-loving households, the Hang-It-All makes for a piece of upbeat wall art as much as a useful device for lifting the detritus of contemporary living off the floor.

## DESIGN FOR ALL AGES

The atomic age was in full swing when Charles and Ray Eames devised this multicolored, wall-mounted coatrack. The Hang-It-All, suitable for hats, jackets, caps, skates, backpacks, handbags, and almost anything else, has not only sustained the test of time, it is just as useful and playful today as it was a half century ago. And, unlike many designs geared toward children, it does not condescend with juvenile tropes. But despite its playful demeanor, the Eames Hang-it-All is infinitely practical. Though it has fourteen separate hooks, the Hang-It-All's compact dimensions make it suitable for even small walls. And the solid maple balls that cap each hook protect sweaters and hats from becoming stretched or distorted.

### PERFECT
Bright, bold colors and sturdy utility characterize Charles and Ray Eames' coatracks. Installed with drywall anchors and screws, they're a perfect way to dress up a bland wall practically.

DIMENSIONS: H 15 IN. (37 CM) x W 20 IN. (50 CM) x D 7 IN. (16.5 CM)

## WHAT MAKES IT CLASSIC

- *ART FOR ART'S SAKE: Given its cheerful demeanor, the wall rack makes for an interesting piece of wall art in and of itself. Consider using it in a hallway or guest bedroom to display your collection of favorite handbags, scarves, or caps.*

- *PRACTICAL: Interesting to look at, the Eames Hang-It-All is also a valuable space saver, offering a compact catchall to keep clutter off the floor.*

- *DESIGNED FOR DELIGHT: The Hang-It-All reflects a proclivity the Eameses had for designing forms as delightful to adults as they are to kids. (In addition to their sophisticated furnishings, the Eameses also crafted children's building blocks, molded plywood animals, patterned spinning tops, and colorful masks.)*

< BOLD STATEMENT
Using the same wooden balls and bold colors that characterize the Eames wall rack, this free-standing coatrack makes a bold statement in any room. Tall and stylish, it's an easy and practical way to add a bit of architectural interest to an expansive space.

# Storage Made Chic

### TRIPLE DUTY

The Eames storage unit can serve triple duty: creating an unobtrusive room divider while working as bookshelves or display space.

DIMENSIONS VARY: AVERAGE LARGE: W 48 IN. (121 CM) X H 59 IN. (149 CM); D 16 IN. (41 CM)

AVERAGE MEDIUM: W 48 IN. (121 CM) X H 33 IN. (83 CM); D 16 IN. (41 CM)

AVERAGE SMALL: W 48 IN. (121 CM) X H 24 IN. (62 CM); D 16 IN. (41 CM)

### WHAT MAKES IT CLASSIC

- *A REAL-LIFE SOLUTION: Timeless and delightful, the Eames storage units can accommodate all kinds of residential detritus in practically any room of the house.*

- *UNDENIABLE CHARM: Blendable with classic midcentury modern furnishings or contemporary designs, the Eames storage units are as fresh looking today as they were when they first came out half a century ago.*

- *A PIECE OF HISTORY: The Eames' many classic designs—from their groundbreaking sofa compact to their many applications of molded plywood—have withstood the test of time, and remain among the finest examples of midcentury modernism.*

Overrun by stuff? Still want style? Fit for the living room, bedroom, dining room, office, or playroom, the hardworking Eames storage unit (ESU) handles everything from action figures to table linens with a chic flair. Though conceived before the advent of VCRs, DVD players, and large-screen TVs, these modern storage units have adapted seamlessly to today's lifestyle needs. From books to dishware, compact discs to clothing, the versatile ESUs make for a strong graphic statement, whatever they hold and wherever they reside

### FLEXIBLE STEEL

Designed by modern masters Charles and Ray Eames in the fifties, the modular system of standardized steel frames with plastic-coated plywood or lacquered Masonite panels and various sliding door and drawer options offers incredible flexibility.

Used as a room divider, cupboard, or desk, the component-based system is available in small, medium, and large units, with natural or tinted wood panels or panels in upbeat primary colors. The large unit has dimpled molded-plywood doors and three drawers; the medium unit has two sliding doors with open shelves; and the small open unit can be used as a shelf or a table. They can be used in singles or multiples to fulfill various storage and spatial needs.

### STYLE THAT WORKS

Mix and match them or use several units in sequence along a wall; they are sure to add a cheerful element to your room, while providing you with a way to organize your clutter. Juxtapose the door colors with a favorite artwork, drapery, or upholstery fabric to visually tie a room together; or choose a neutral wood, tan, or gray finish to blend in with a more subdued environment. With their charming good looks, endless flexibility, and pure attention to function, these classic storage units can solve storage problems with style in any room.

∧ SENSE OF INTIMACY
A block of Eames storage units define this conversation area, creating a sense of intimacy in a large space. The colorful panels provide a bold accent, complementing the artwork and contrasting with the sleek, monochromatic furnishings.

< UNOBTRUSIVE
Strategically placed Eames create an unobtrusive room divider in this modern studio. Notice how the screened sections create a visual border without blocking natural light.

< CALM, MATHEMATICAL
The vivid color and bold graphic form of the
Cross cabinet make a striking statement in this
bathroom. The calm, mathematical geometry of
the tile walls contrasts with the urgency of the
Red Cross.

# A Touch of the Unusual

**DESIGN STATEMENT**
Executed in bright-red metal, Thomas Eriksson's Cross cabinet offers extra storage space and a big design statement. This cabinet is a real attention getter.

DIMENSIONS: VARY

**WHAT MAKES IT CLASSIC**

- *DESIGNED TO SURPRISE: Consider the bold Cross cabinet for any space short on storage and decorative flair. The graphic piece provides a shock of unexpected color, lending a sense of fun to even the most staid environments.*

- *SYMBOLIC INSPIRATION: A designer of corporate logos as well as spaces, Eriksson came up with the Cross cabinet for Cappellini's Progetto-Ogetto in 1992. "The idea was to turn a recognizable two-dimensional symbol into a useful everyday object," Eriksson explains.*

Some accessories support a greater design but would go unnoticed on their own. Others jump right out at you. Swedish designer and architect Thomas Eriksson's Cross cabinet is definitely in the latter camp. Rendered completely in metal, the industrial-looking Cross cabinet creates a strong, graphic statement, adding a splash of color to monochromatic walls. This cabinet offers necessary storage space while creating a definitive artistic statement.

**FIRST AID FOR YOUR WALLS**
The Red Cross graphic was well-suited to this design, given its association with rescue. "You need to be able to find your first-aid kit fast when you need it," Eriksson says. "Producing a monochromatic red cabinet in the form of a cross allowed us to create an object that indicates its meaning quickly."

Useful in the bathroom, hallway, office, kitchen, or workshop, the Cross cabinet creates a strong graphic form wherever it is hung. Suitable for keeping Band-Aids, antiseptic cream, headache pills, or your favorite bottle of twelve-year-old scotch, the cabinet communicates "help can be found here" with a vivid directness that is anything but somber.

# Architecture to Go

When space cries out for a bit more intimacy, interest, and texture, the Eames folding screen can save the day. Used as a room divider, privacy screen, or simply as a piece of artwork in and of itself, the Eames folding plywood screen is a masterpiece of design that can add drama to any space.

**GROUNDBREAKING**

Sculptural and simple, this stunning screen is an excellent example of the Eameses' work with molded plywood. Created through groundbreaking techniques they developed themselves, this screen testifies to the Eameses' devotion to simple, useful forms.

**CHOOSE YOUR FUNCTION**

This versatile piece can serve as a backdrop for other furnishings or artworks, or function simply as a separator in a large, multiuse area. Its subtle, sculptural form adds visual interest to a space that lacks architectural details, and creates vertical height in rooms dominated by low, horizontal planes. The screen's sophisticated design and neutral materials blend well with objects and furniture of various styles, and lend a lovely softness to hard-edged interiors without being cloying.

DIMENSIONS: H 68 IN. (173 CM) X D .5 IN. (5.7 CM) X W 60 IN. (152 CM)

Durable and extremely portable, the Eames screen can be moved about the home to meet changing needs and create different decorative effects. Use it to hide a home computer in the corner of your living room or bedroom, to camouflage a guest bed in the attic, or create a separate play area for children (and their toys) in the family room. Orient the screen perpendicular to your front door to create a virtual hallway that separates the entryway from your living area. Use it to separate the kitchen from the dining area when you entertain. Graze it from above with steeply angled track or pot lights to create a dramatic effect at night.

**WHAT MAKES IT CLASSIC**

- *A TRADEMARK PIECE: Molding plywood into complex curves was a hallmark of many of the designs of Charles and Ray Eames, the midcentury duo whose works have become seminal examples of American modernism.*

- *VERSATILITY IN FORM AND FUNCTION: With a stunning, sculptural form and a variety of uses, this a piece that easily becomes the centerpiece of any interior and redefines itself based on the job it is set out to do. Yet it is totally portable and can folds away compactly when not in use.*

- *A SCREEN FOR EVERYONE: Originally crafted in rosewood, the Eames screen is now available in cherry, walnut, or ash veneer with a maple core.*

∧ SENSE OF MOVEMENT
Adding a bit of textural interest to a rather
monolithic rear wall, the Eames folding screen
lends a sense of movement to this interesting
but somewhat narrow space. The screen's fluid
form echoes the sculptural shape of the
Noguchi coffee table, while the molded
plywood form complements the Eames-
designed side chairs.

∧ SCULPTURAL FORM
The Savoy vase's signature shape makes creating stunning flower arrangements easy, but its sculptural form creates a beautiful statement all on its own. Placed alone on a simple side table, the vase becomes a centerpiece in and of itself.

# Cool, Complex Curves

## UNEXPECTED DIRECTION

Echoing the designer's work in bent plywood, Alvar Aalto's classic Savoy vase takes a familiar material in an entirely new and unexpected direction. The vase's fluid lines seem almost natural in form, and work in almost any interior, from rigidly formal to casual and eclectic.

DIMENSIONS: H 6.25 IN. (15 CM) X D 8 IN. (20 CM)

## WHAT MAKES IT CLASSIC

- *ABSOLUTELY ORIGINAL: One of the most interesting aspects of the Savoy series is that the walls of the blow-molded vases vary in depth. As a result, no two vases are exactly alike.*

- *SURREALIST INFLUENCE: Aalto was said to be a fan of such surrealist artists as Jean Arp and Joan Miro, and his abstracted, biomorphic forms can be compared to some of the elements in their most famous works. The glass forms were exhibited in Paris in 1937, winning Aalto and Karhula-Iitala, the vases' manufacturer, international acclaim.*

Originally produced in clear, brown, azure blue, green, and smoke-colored glass, Alvar Aalto's 1936 Savoy vase (named for the Helsinki hotel also designed by Aalto) continues to create a sublime statement in contemporary homes, whether holding flowers, river stones, popcorn, or nothing at all. The sculpted, organic shapes of these free-form vases add an artistic touch to the bedroom, the dining room, the foyer, the kitchen, and even the bathroom. The Savoy lends elegance wherever it lands.

### THE PERFECT VASE

Aalto's vase may be high art, but it serves more humble purposes with exceptional grace. It is the perfect vessel for casual flower arrangements, making a large statement with the addition of just a few carefully chosen stems: A single sunflower, a pair of large-headed mums, or a trio of peonies or old roses make a stunning centerpiece or accent without depleting your entire garden. Alternatively, a grower's bunch of single-variety tulips fills the vase with a harmonious blend of graceful, straight stems and rounded flower heads that are at once organic and architectural.

### THE SHAPE OF THINGS

Like his many designs in bent plywood, Finnish architect Alvar Aalto's glass forms are sublimely organic in form. Legend has it that the curvaceous shape of Aalto's signature vase was inspired by the folds of an Eskimo woman's leather trousers, and by the jagged shorelines of the Finnish fjords. The unexpected form creates a sense of movement and rhythm absent in traditional symmetrical vases and adds an unexpected dash of character to spare, linear interiors. In a formal foyer, it is a foil for the seriousness of staid antiques. Or fill it with fresh-cut basil and place it on a kitchen counter, where it will serve both culinary needs and aesthetic desires.

# Photo Credits

Alvar Aalto/Artek, 70; 71
Ed Addeo/Donghia Furniture and Textiles Ltd., 63
Designed by Harry Allen for Dune, 84
Courtesy of Anglepoise Co., 99 (top)
Rachel Ashwell/Shabby Chic, 36; 37
Courtesy of Baker Furniture, 20; 21; 64; 65; 76; 77
Courtesy of Best & Lloyd, Ltd., 111
Antoine Bootz, 9; 58
Björg, 29; 39
Cappellini/Thomas Eriksson Arkitekter, 134; 135
Courtesy of Cassina, USA, 46; 48; 49; 55
Christies Images, 41
Courtesy of designaddict.com, 125; 129
Courtesy of Design Within Reach, 16; 24; 28; 107; 108; 112; 116; 124; 127; 131
Courtesy of Desiron, 95
Pieter Estersohn, 25; 27 (bottom); 43; 47; 85 (both); 86
European Furniture Importers, 42
Courtesy of The Futon Shop, 80
John Hall, 90; 133 (bottom)
Ken Hayden/The Interior Archive, 110
Courtesy of Hickory Chair Co., 50; 51
Courtesy of Hickory Chair/Thomas O'Brien Collection, 60; 61
Courtesy of Hinson/Hanson Co., 100
Courtesy of Vladimir Kagan Design Group, 33
Courtesy of Knoll, 44; 45; 56
Christian Korab, 10; 57; 121
Udo Kowalsky Kaslov Studio/Louis Poulsen Lighting, 104; 105 (top); 105 (middle right)
Courtesy of Lexington Furniture, 93
Courtesy of Maine Cottage Furniture, 79; 87
©Homes & Gardens/John Mason/IPC Media Ltd., 98; 99 (bottom)
Lynn Massimo, 32
James Merrell, 62
Courtesy of Herman Miller, Inc., 34; 132; 136
Courtesy of The Museum of Modern Art, 59; 67; 115; 117 (top left); 138; 139
Courtesy of Old Timber Table Company, 68
Orrefors, 123
Courtesy of Pottery Barn, 78; 94 (right)
©Ray Reiss, 120
Eric Roth, 22; 26 (top); 69; 101 (top right & bottom); 102; 103; 105 (bottom); 130
Paul Rocheleau, 40
Paul Rocheleau/Courtesy of Thos. Moser Cabinetmakers, 72; 73;
Eric Staudenmaier/Beate Works, 18
Courtesy of Stickley, 38; 92
Tim Street-Porter/Beate Works, 35; 89; 94 (left); 101 (top left); 133 (top)
Knut E. Svensson, 121
Courtesy of Tekno, Italy, 19; 23
Edna van der Wyck/The Interior Archive, 81
Design by Massimo Vignelli/Heller, Inc., 128
Fritz von der Schulenburg/The Interior Archive, 113 (top left)
Paul Warchol, 17 (top); 54; 105 (middle left); 106 (both); 109; 113 (top right & bottom); 114; 117 (bottom); 137
Courtesy of Waterbeds UK, 82; 83
Brandon Webster, 66; 126
Wegner, Produced by PP Mobler, Denmark, 27
Courtesy of Eldred Wheeler, 88; 91
Andrew Wood/The Interior Archive, 17 (bottom)

# Resources

ANGLEPOISE LAMP
Anglepoise
England
www.anglepoise.co.uk

TIZIO LAMP
Artemide, Inc.
Farmingdale, New York
www.tizio.com

L-LEG TABLE
Artek oy ab
Helsinki, Finland
info@artek.fi

OVAL X-BACK CHAIR
ARCHETYPE DINING TABLE
SLEIGH BED
Baker Furniture
A Division of Kohler Co.
Grand Rapids, Michigan
www.bakerfurniture.com

BESTLITE
Best & Lloyd, Ltd.
Smethwick, West Midland, England
www.bestandlloyd.co.uk

CROSS CABINET
Cappellini Modernage
Milan, Italy
www.capellini.it

SECTIONAL SOFA
NEST SOFA
THE ALLEN TABLE
Cassina, USA
New York, New York
www.cassinausa.com

THONET BENTWOOD CHAIR
CLUB CHAIR
EAMES PLYWOOD DINING CHAIR
COSTANZA LAMP
BRERA PENDANT LAMP
BERENICE LAMP
AKARI LAMP
ROUND-UP STORAGE SYSTEM
ATOMIC WALL CLOCK
EAMES HANG-IT-ALL
Design Within Reach
Oakland, California
www.dwr.com

ROUND-UP STORAGE SYSTEM
HELLERWARE
Designaddict.com
Brussels, Belgium
www.designaddict.com

IRON BED
Desiron
New York, New York
www.desiron.com

D'URSO SUPPER TABLE
Donghia Furniture/Textiles, Ltd.

New York, New York
www.donghia.com

MURPHY BED
Dune
New York, New York
www.dune-ny.com

LE CORBUSIER GRAND CONFORT SOFA
European Furniture Importers
Chicago, Illinois
www.eurofurniture.com

FUTON
The Futon Shop
San Francisco, California
www.thefutonshop.com

HELLERWARE
Heller, Inc.
New York, New York
www.helleronline.com

CAMELBACK SOFA
WOOSTER TRAY TABLE
Hickory Chair
Hickory, North Carolina
www.hickorychair.com

HANSEN SWING-ARM LAMP
Hinson & Company
Long Island City, New York
(212) 475-4100

FREE-FORM SERPENTINE SOFA
The Vladimir Kagan Design Group
New York, New York
www.vladimirkagan.com

FLORENCE KNOLL SOFA
EERO SAARINEN PEDESTAL TABLE
AKARI
Knoll
New York, New York
www.knoll.com

DAYBED
TRUNDLE BED
Maine Cottage Furniture
Yarmouth, Maine
www.mainecottage.com

EAMES SOFA COMPACT
EAMES HANG-IT-ALL
EAMES FOLDING SCREEN
EAMES STORAGE UNIT
Herman Miller
Zeeland, Michigan
www.hermanmiller.com

PEACOCK CHAIR
PP Mobler ApS.
Allerod, Denmark
www.ppdk.com

SHAKER TABLE
Thos. Moser Cabinetmakers

Auburn, Maine
www.thosmoser.com

EILEEN GRAY ADJUSTABLE TABLE
NOGUCHI COFFEE TABLE
BAUHAUS TABLE LAMP
SAVOY VASE
Museum of Modern Art Design Store
New York, New York
www.moma.org

FARM TABLE
Old Timber Table Company
Dallas, Texas
www.oldtimbertable.com

IRON BED
Pottery Barn
San Francisco, California
www.potterybarn.com

INGEBARD RAMAN DECANTER AND DRINK-
ING GLASSES
Royal Scandinavia
Berlin, New Jersey
www.royalscanusa.com

SHABBY CHIC SOFA
Shabby Chic
Los Angeles, California
www.shabbychic.com

THE STICKLEY SETTLE
BUNK BEDS
L. & J. G. Stickley, Inc.
Manlius, New York
www.stickley.com

PH SERIES LAMPS
Louis Poulsen Lighting
Sluseholmen, Denmark
www.louis-poulsen.com

MIES VAN DER ROHE BARCELONA CHAIR
CESCA CHAIR
MIES VAN DER ROHE SOFA
Tekno
Barberino Val D'Elsa, Italy
www.tekno-italy.it

WATERBED
Waterbeds, UK
Sutton, England
www.onlywaterbeds.com

CANOPY BED
FOUR-POST BED
Eldred Wheeler
Hingham, Massachusetts
www.eldredwheeler.com

TOWN AND COUNTRY SALT AND PEPPER
SHAKERS
World of Ceramics
Morganton, North Carolina
Collector's information:
www.mindspring.com/~dway/town.html

# Index

# Acknowledgments

I would like to extend my thanks to the contributing writers, designers, and manufacturers who helped develop and shape this book.

# About the Author

Elana Frankel, formerly a senior editor at *Interior Design* magazine, has written on architecture and design for *surface, Architectural Record, Metropolis, I.D., Grid,* and *Home.* In addition, she is a frequent lecturer and panelist both in the United States and abroad. She resides in New York City.